# THE ORLANDO
# CEPEDA
## STORY

## BRUCE MARKUSEN

Piñata Books
Arte Público Press
Houston, Texas

This volume is made possible through grants from the Andrew W. Mellon Foundation and the City of Houston through The Cultural Arts Council of Houston, Harris County.

*Piñata Books are full of surprises!*

Piñata Books

An imprint of
Arte Público Press
University of Houston
452 Cullen Performance Hall
Houston, Texas 77204-2174

Cover design Ken Bullock
Cover photo courtesy of San Francisco Giants/Archives

Markusen, Bruce.
    The Orlando Cepeda Story / by Bruce Markusen.
        p.   cm.
    Includes bibliographical references (p.) and index.
    ISBN 1-55885-333-2
    1. Cepeda, Orlando.   2. Baseball players—Puerto Rico—Biography.
    I. Title.
    GV865.C4 M37 2001
    796.357'092—dc21
    [B]                                                     00-065258
                                                            CIP

♾ The paper used in this publication meets the requirements of the American National Standard for Information Sciences—Permanence of Paper for Printed Library Materials, ANSI Z39.48-1984.

1 2 3 4 5 6 7 8 9 0            10 9 8 7 6 5 4 3 2 1

*This book is dedicated to Rosa Miranda,
who always showed care and love in
raising me from my youngest days.*

*Thank you, Rosa.*

# Contents

# Introduction

Orlando Cepeda has experienced one of the most storied lives in baseball history. During his six stops in the major leagues, he played with sixteen Hall of Famers, a simply remarkable total. The lengthy list of legends included Hank Aaron and Willie Mays, arguably the two greatest players of the 1960s, and Bob Gibson and Juan Marichal, two of the era's hallmark pitchers.

While many Hall of Famers played for only two or three teams during their careers, Cepeda lived a far more diversified baseball life. In 1958, he made his major league debut with the San Francisco Giants, the first of his half-dozen big league teams. During his nine-year stay in the Bay Area, he played with future National League president Bill White and four eventual members of the Hall of Fame: Marichal, Mays, Willie McCovey, and Gaylord Perry. A trade in the middle of the 1966 season sent him to the St. Louis Cardinals, where he played with the Hall of Fame likes of Gibson, Lou Brock, and Steve Carlton, and became friendly with such notables as Curt Flood, Roger Maris, and Tim McCarver. Flood ended up challenging baseball's controversial reserve clause, which indirectly led to the start of free agency. Maris held the record for most home runs in a single season until Mark McGwire and Sammy Sosa came along. And McCarver went on to become one of the most successful broadcasters in baseball.

After a short stint in St. Louis, the Cardinals traded Cepeda to the Atlanta Braves for Joe Torre, a fine player who would become even more famous as the manager of the world champion New York Yankees. Cepeda batted behind Hank Aaron in a stacked Braves' lineup, while also offering support to the team's knuckleballing right-handers Phil Niekro and Hoyt Wilhelm. In 1972, chronic knee problems and a dispute with Atlanta management led to a trade to the Oakland A's—this time in exchange for a talented but troubled pitcher named Denny McLain. Although Cepeda came to bat only a few times for the A's, he did share roster space with three more legends of the game: Reggie Jackson, Jim "Catfish" Hunter, and Rollie Fingers. While in Oakland, he also played for one of the era's most successful managers (Dick Williams) and perhaps its most controversial owner (Charlie Finley).

Just when his career seemed at a standstill, the Boston Red Sox signed Cepeda to be their first designated hitter, allowing him to play a full season with the likes of Luis Aparicio, Carlton "Pudge" Fisk, and Carl Yastrzemski. The following year, a surprising spring training release led to his final major league stop—the Kansas City Royals. Just as Cepeda was saying good-bye to the game, he was also saying hello to a player named George Brett, a rookie third baseman struggling to find his way. Brett would become one of the greatest hitters of his era on his way to entering the Hall of Fame.

Having played with and against so many well-known players, Orlando Cepeda has seen just about everything during his career in baseball. Off the field, he encountered an even wider range of experiences: poverty, racism, culture shock, drug problems, prison, several marriages, and a life-changing religious conversion. Through it all, he continued to learn about others—and himself. His story—as rich and full as it has been—is one that we can learn from, too.

# Chapter One

# Birth of The Baby Bull

Pedro Aníbal "Perucho" Cepeda was one of the finest-hitting shortstops to play on the island of Puerto Rico. He twice led the Puerto Rican Winter League in batting. In 1941, he hit .423 while leading the league in runs batted in (RBIs). The following season, he connected at a .464 clip, a simply remarkable batting average. He won several home run titles. He hit the ball so powerfully that some people called him the "Babe Ruth of Puerto Rico," or the "Babe Ruth of the Caribbean." Pedro grew into such a fearsome hitter that the New York Cubans, a well-respected team in the old Negro Leagues, repeatedly recruited him to play for them. The dark-skinned Cepeda said no. He didn't like the racial conditions that existed on the United States mainland. He didn't feel it was fair to exclude black players from performing in the major leagues, a situation that existed until 1947.

As a result, Pedro continued to play on the island. He remained a devastating hitter, even into his forties. And even playing against major league competition. One year, the New York Yankees visited Puerto Rico to play a series of exhibition games. Pedro Cepeda had to face Allie Reynolds and Vic Raschi, two of the top pitchers in the American League. In four at-bats against Reynolds and Raschi, the forty-something Cepeda stroked four consecutive hits.

As he grew older, Cepeda also maintained his competitive streak, which was legendary on the island. So deter-

1

mined to win, Pedro once pulled off an amazing play that still seems unbelievable to this day. With a man at third base and one out, Pedro sensed that the other team was planning a "squeeze" bunt to bring the runner home. As the pitch was delivered, Pedro charged in from his position at shortstop. Sure enough, the batter laid down the bunt as the runner from third raced home. Pedro pounced on the bunt and tagged the runner, whom he had beaten to the plate. Not hesitating for a moment, he then spun his body and fired the ball to first base. The throw beat the batter to the base, completing the double play. Simply incredible.

Fans and friends of Pedro called him "Perucho," a Spanish nickname that has no literal translation or meaning in English. They also called him "The Bull" because of his stocky, five-foot, eleven-inch, 200-pound build and his ability to hit the ball with power into the outfield gaps. So, it was only natural that his son would draw the nickname "The Baby Bull." Yet, no one could have known that Perucho Cepeda's son would become even more famous in the United States than his legendary father.

On September 17, 1937, "The Baby Bull" was born in the city of Ponce. Perucho and his wife Carmen named their boy Manuel Orlando Cepeda y Pennes. (Pennes was the maiden name of Orlando's mother; in Puerto Rico, it is customary to attach the mother's maiden name to the child's last name.) In common everyday use, the name would be shortened to Orlando Cepeda. It was a beautiful name, one that flowed from the lips. *Orlando Cepeda.*

From the start, the elder Cepeda stressed discipline in raising his son. "He was very demanding, very strict," Orlando said of his father in a 1973 interview with *Black Sports Magazine.* "His word was law in our house." Perucho wanted to make sure that all members of his family lived a healthy lifestyle. "He did not drink or smoke," Orlando said, "and he made sure no one in our family did either."

Orlando's father also had a bad temper. When his children did not behave properly, he let them know about it—loudly. Perucho also lost his temper playing baseball. He demanded perfection from himself as a player. When he was less than perfect on the ballfield, he became mad at himself. He hated to lose, so much so that he often didn't talk for hours after games. After one particularly tough loss, Perucho was so upset that he boarded the wrong bus. His two sons, who were riding with him, didn't dare tell him about the mistake that he had made. "We were too scared to say anything," Orlando told Myron Cope of *Sport Magazine* in 1962. "We just sat there and kept riding."

Perucho often showed his anger and his mood swings, but that didn't keep him from being a popular person on the island. "Despite his temper, my father had a great personality," Orlando told Lennie Megliola of *Black Sports Magazine.* "Everybody loved him." Orlando saw evidence of that whenever he traveled downtown with his father. "Every few seconds someone would stop us and talk to him. They all idolized him; they wanted to buy him something."

The generosity of others helped out the Cepedas, who were a poor family that moved from city to city, usually living in slum-like houses. After all, Perucho made only a few dollars a week playing baseball. Some of that money never even made it into the Cepeda house because of Perucho's unfortunate gambling habit. He often lost large amounts of his salary making bets, when the family could have used the money on food and other important household items.

In spite of the family's poverty, Perucho had a number of famous friends. Josh Gibson and Satchel Paige, two of the greatest players in the history of the Negro Leagues, used to visit the Cepeda house. With people like that in the Cepeda living room, it was no wonder that Orlando learned about baseball at a young age. He listened to the conversations between his father and his friends, who liked to talk about baseball during visits to the Cepeda house. The discussions intrigued Orlando, who soon became a fan of the game.

Yet, Perucho Cepeda did not want to force baseball on his young son. He decided not to take him to very many games at local ballparks. He wanted Orlando to develop an interest in baseball on his own.

So Orlando usually went to ballgames by himself. He eventually started playing baseball in local youth leagues. Filled with pride, Perucho started telling people that his son would become an even better player than he was. Unfortunately, Orlando also began hearing negative comparisons to his legendary father. Too many people told him that he would never be as good a player as Perucho.

The putdowns discouraged Orlando from playing ball, just as they had discouraged his older brother, Pedro, a few years earlier. Orlando turned to a new interest, the sport of basketball. In time, that became his favorite sport to play. Baseball moved well into the background.

The teenaged Orlando played basketball exceptionally well. At six-foot-two, he was strong and athletic, and tough to handle near the basket. One day, Orlando was playing basketball when he leapt for a rebound. As he jumped and landed, he felt a pain in his right knee. Orlando had torn cartilage in the knee. The injury would have to be repaired through surgery.

This was not the first time that Orlando had experienced problems with his legs. He had actually been born with a deformity in his right leg, which was bowed instead of straight. As a result, his right foot pointed inward instead of straight ahead.

In repairing the knee, the doctor intentionally broke a bone in Orlando's leg, just below his knee. He then reset the foot in its proper position. Although the procedure straightened out his leg and corrected the positioning of his foot, it would force Orlando to stay in the hospital for two months and prevent him from playing any sports for a full year. The doctor also told Orlando's father that his son would not be able to pursue a professional career in sports. If he put too much stress on the leg, he could reinjure it at any time.

While Orlando was out of action, he put on weight, going from 130 pounds to 170 pounds in a matter of months. The added muscle figured to help him become a stronger hitter in baseball—if he were to return to the game, that is. He was still showing a preference for playing basketball.

One day, he went to visit a friend who was playing in a sandlot game in the San Juan area. Orlando intended only to watch but he decided to pick up a bat during the visit and take some swings. He found himself hitting the ball harder than he ever had.

Orlando decided to stop playing basketball, which required more running and jumping and put more stress on his knees. He chose to return to his first love—baseball. Joining a standout amateur baseball team, Cepeda led the club to the Puerto Rican championship.

By now, Orlando's father had begun to follow his son's pursuit of baseball. Perucho offered his son some advice. He told Orlando to concentrate on one of his three main interests, whether it was baseball, basketball, or playing the drums, which he also loved to do. *Pick one and become the best you can be at it.*

His father influenced his decision heavily. "One day, he came home and saw me playing basketball, and threw everything away," Orlando recalls. "Baseball or nothing," Perucho declared to his youngest son. "He threw away my basketball, threw everything [all of the basketball equipment] out of my house."

With his father providing him definite direction, Orlando forgot about becoming a professional basketball player, or a drummer. He now dreamed of becoming a baseball player. His father tried to help him, but not by teaching him the game, which he felt had to come naturally. Instead, Perucho tried to *motivate* his son, often by yelling at him when he made mistakes. On more than one occasion, the elder Cepeda left his seat in the stands and stormed over to a fence that bordered the playing field. He began shouting at Orlando, chastising him for making a play the wrong way. "I remember one time we spent all night talking about fundamentals," Orlando recalls. "We talked about a play—a rundown—'if this happened, you have to do this.' The next day, the same play came up in a game, so I did it the wrong way. Right there, in the middle of the ballgame, he chewed me out."

Cepeda remembers another incident involving his demanding father. "We were playing an important game, for the championship of Puerto Rico in amateur ball. There was a fly ball. I dropped it. I struck out two times. He came down to the field and said, 'You got two more times [at bat]. If you don't do anything, you don't come home tonight.' He mean it. *He mean it.*" It was certainly a tough way for a young man to play baseball, but it seemed to make the young Cepeda a better player.

Orlando eventually realized that he would have to leave the island to pursue his dream of playing baseball professionally. He wanted to play the best baseball competition in the world. Although Puerto Rico had an excellent winter baseball league, it was not the best. The best baseball was played in the major leagues, which were located on the mainland of the United States. That was Orlando's desired destination.

Scouts from major league teams eventually came to watch Orlando play. They were impressed by his size and his ability to hit with power. They also noticed something unusual about him. Although he was a big kid who stood six feet, two inches tall, and looked a bit overweight at 205 pounds, he had nimble feet and could run. He had rare athletic ability.

Veteran baseball scout Pedro "Pedrín" Zorrilla soon became aware of Cepeda's talent. Zorrilla owned the Santurce Cangrejeros (Crabbers), a team in the Puerto Rican Winter League. He also served as a scout for the New York Giants, a major league team. Zorrilla often recommended young Latino players to the Giants, who were always on the lookout for new talent.

Zorrilla also knew a little bit about the Cepeda family, having watched Orlando's father star for his team in Santurce several years earlier. Zorrilla had asked Perucho for his permission to hire Orlando as the team's batboy in 1953–54—the same winter that legendary players Roberto Clemente and Willie Mays played for the Crabbers. Perucho said yes, giving Orlando his first taste of professional baseball and allowing him to associate with a team that featured the youngster's boyhood hero, pitcher Rubén Gómez.

Zorrilla watched the younger Cepeda play an exhibition game against a Dominican all-star team. The Dominicans provided substantial competition that day, considering that they had future major leaguers Felipe Alou and Julián Javier on their roster. Although Zorrilla was actually more interested in scouting a promising Puerto Rican infielder named José Pagán, he certainly took note of Cepeda that day. Orlando played very well, going 4-for-5 with a home run against the Dominicans.

Zorrilla came away so impressed that he arranged a tryout for Cepeda and four other young Puerto Ricans with the New York Giants. The contingent of hopefuls, which included future major leaguers Cepeda, Pagán, and pitcher Julio Navarro, made the four-hour flight from San Juan to Miami, Florida. Unable to speak English and ask for help, the players missed the first bus from Miami that was scheduled to take them to the city of Melbourne, where the Giants held the tryout. As a result, the players arrived at Melbourne between four and five o'clock in the morning. With no one awake at such an early hour, the young men settled into the Giants' minor league barracks.

A man awoke the Puerto Rican hopefuls after only two hours of sleep. He told them that they were in the wrong part of the barracks. They would have to move up to the second floor, where the black players stayed. It was a rude welcome to the world of segregation.

Accompanied by little sleep and surrounded by strangers, Cepeda now had to do his best to impress the Giants. Fortunately, Orlando was not completely alone in his mission. A man named Dave García, one of the managers in the Giants' minor league system, reached out to help Orlando. García spoke Spanish, which enabled him to communicate with Cepeda and the other Latino players. García often went up to their rooms to play cards with them, and gave them encouraging words of advice.

Cepeda showed good power at the tryout, but the other parts of his game failed to impress the Giants. Still, they decided to offer Cepeda a contract, which included a small $500 bonus. Compared to what top young players in other organizations had been offered, it was not a lot of money. But it was Cepeda's only offer.

Orlando had a choice to make. He could continue his career in Puerto Rico and hope for a better offer. Or he could say yes to the Giants. Even though he was barely past high school age, Orlando decided to sign the contract. As the boy prepared to leave Puerto Rico for his new job in the states, Pedrín Zorrilla gave him some advice. "Pay no mind to injustices, keep your temper in your pocket, remember Jackie Robinson, and go out and hustle." With those words in mind, Orlando Cepeda left his home in Puerto Rico and headed for the States.

# Chapter Two

# Land of Segregation

On the surface, signing with the New York Giants seemed glamorous. After all, they were one of baseball's most famous teams and played in the largest city in the United States. But Orlando wasn't heading directly to New York. He wasn't ready to play in the major leagues just yet. He would have to start out in the low minor leagues.

There was one problem with that plan. Racial segregation, which existed throughout much of the South during the 1950s, discouraged some teams from having dark-skinned African American or Latin American players. The Giants needed to find a minor league team that would accept black players, but they weren't finding any takers for Cepeda.

In fact, the Giants were having such trouble placing Cepeda with a minor league team that they thought about releasing him. After all, he was not considered a top-flight prospect. If he were to be released, it would be no great loss. Or so the Giants thought.

A man named Alex Pómpez, the owner of a team in the Negro Leagues and a father figure to many black players, fought to save Cepeda's career. As an advisor to the Giants, he told them they would be making a mistake if they released Cepeda. Pómpez knew about a minor league team that needed a third baseman, which was Cepeda's main position. The team played in Salem (Virginia) in the Class-D Appalachian League.

It took Orlando three days and three nights of traveling by bus to reach his new team. Salem was also a long way from the major leagues—six full levels, to be exact. Orlando had much work to do in proving to the Giants that he could eventually help them in a National League pennant race.

Just before the start of the regular season, Orlando's family called him back to Puerto Rico. He needed to come to the bedside of his father, who was seriously ill with malaria. Perucho had contracted the disease while working for the local water department. In performing maintenance work, he often found himself up to his hips in cold, unsanitary water.

For weeks, Perucho had refused to see a doctor. He had also been lax in taking his medicine regularly. He was now lying in bed at his home, in a coma, and very close to death. Just days before Orlando's first scheduled game, Perucho Cepeda died. He was only forty-nine years old, and only four years removed from his last game as a baseball player. In order to help pay the costs of his father's funeral, Orlando used the $500 bonus that he had received from the Giants.

The timing of a death in the family, while never good, could not have been worse. With Orlando heading to the States, his brother Pedro stationed in the military, and Mrs. Cepeda back in Puerto Rico, the surviving members of the Cepeda family were isolated from one another. They would have little chance to comfort each other at a time of tragedy and need.

Orlando thought about staying in Puerto Rico, but his mother, Carmen, would have none of it. She reminded him that there were no jobs waiting for him on the island. More importantly, she told him that he couldn't fulfill his dream of playing in the major leagues by staying at home.

With Perucho gone, Carmen assumed even more responsibility in guiding her youngest son. "Right after my father died," Orlando says, "my mother took the roles of father and mother. I was very lucky." Although Carmen was very small at four feet, eleven inches, she was tough and feisty, and a good, strong influence on Orlando.

Having discussed the situation with his mother, Orlando returned to the States but played poorly for Salem at the start of the season. The loss of his father had left him in a daze. "I was really too upset to play. It took me two months to get over his death," Cepeda told *Black Sports Magazine* in 1973. "He had always wanted to see me play as a pro." Because of his untimely death, Perucho Cepeda never had the opportunity to watch his son play ball in the United States.

Other obstacles awaited Orlando. During a road trip to Iowa, Salem's team bus stopped at a restaurant along the highway. The restaurant refused to serve Cepeda, who was black. The restaurant owners had a policy: they served only white people. This policy of segregation, although racist and unfair, was perfectly legal in 1955. Orlando would have to wait on the bus while his teammates sat comfortably in the diner. He would also have to deal with segregated dining cars on trains and segregated seating in movie theaters.

Cepeda had been warned about this kind of treatment by another player, Roberto Clemente of the Pittsburgh Pirates. Like Cepeda, Clemente was black and Puerto Rican. Roberto had arrived on the United States mainland just a year before Orlando. He knew all about segregation. He knew it would be no different for Cepeda.

Even so, Clemente's words alone couldn't prepare Cepeda for a culture that was so different from Puerto Rico. When Orlando walked the streets in southern towns and cities, he heard some people call him racist names. "Nigger," an unacceptable word in the English language today, was one of them. Even at the ballpark, Cepeda heard the word being shouted at him by some mean-spirited fans. "When I came here, I ran into the race problem," Cepeda told Stan Isaacs of *Newsday* many years later. "We didn't have that in Puerto Rico. I wasn't used to it." At times, Cepeda thought about leaving the States and heading back to Puerto Rico, where people treated him better. He thought about quitting many times, but each time he decided against it.

Unfortunately, the team in Salem had no other Latin players. Cepeda was left alone as he tried to deal with racism. None of his teammates, coaches, or even his manager offered him any help.

Cepeda's problems went beyond racism, too. He knew very little English, which made it difficult for him to communicate with his teammates, or do simple things like order food in restaurants. He couldn't understand what was written on the menu. As a result, he did most of his eating in cafeterias, where he could point to food that was displayed in assembly-line fashion.

All in all, Cepeda felt miserable. He also played poorly, batting only .247, with one home run in twenty-six games. He wrote a letter to Pedrín Zorrilla, asking him for help.

When Salem released Cepeda, Zorrilla and Dave García stepped in to provide some help. They worked out a deal to have Cepeda play for a team in Kokomo, Indiana. Like Salem, Kokomo was a lower-level Class-D minor league team. Even worse, it was located in an area of the country where the racist Ku Klux Klan was quite prominent.

Even though the move hardly seemed like an answer to his problems, it was actually the best thing that could have happened to Cepeda. In Kokomo, Cepeda met a man named Walt Dixon. He was the manager of Kokomo and also the team's star first baseman. Unlike the manager and players in Salem, Dixon tried to help Cepeda. Knowing that his rookie third baseman was facing unfair treatment, Dixon tried to encourage him whenever possible. Even though Orlando slumped from time to time, Dixon continued to believe in him.

Dixon made life easier for Orlando, who finally felt that someone was on his side. Cepeda played for Kokomo the rest of the season. In ninety-two games, he belted 21 homers and piled up 91 RBIs. In spite of a late-season slump, he batted an incredible .393, which was good enough to lead the league. After his early-season struggles, Orlando had arrived as a professional ballplayer.

The following season, the Giants reacquired Cepeda from Kokomo and assigned him to their Class-C team in St. Cloud, Minnesota. Orlando's new manager, Charlie Fox, gave him a nickname. He called him "Plo Plo," which means "fat boy" in English. Although that name might have sounded like an insult, Fox actually meant it in a playful way. He liked Cepeda, even if he was a little bit on the pudgy side.

Fox liked the way Cepeda hit the ball even better. Cepeda led all hitters in the Northern League with a .355 average, giving him his second straight batting championship. He also led the league in home runs and RBIs, which gave him one of baseball's rarest accomplishments—the "Triple Crown." Thankfully, Cepeda also switched positions. Fox wisely decided to move him from third base, where he appeared clumsy and unsure, to first base, where he fielded smoothly and confidently. Orlando played so well in the field and at the plate that the Giants moved him up several classifications in 1957—all the way to the American Association, rated as Class-AAA (Triple-A). That put him just one level away from his ultimate goal: playing in the major leagues.

Cepeda started out poorly for the Minneapolis Millers, who considered demoting him to a lower minor league. With Minneapolis primed to send him down, Orlando saved himself by going 4-for-4 one day. It was a sign of good things to come. Cepeda would go on to bat .309 with 25 home runs and 108 RBIs. His fielding also continued to get better. All of this improvement came at the right time for Orlando's mother, who finally saw him play for the first time. "I had to beg her to go to the game," Orlando told Myron Cope of *Sport Magazine* in a 1962 interview. Carmen had always stayed away from Orlando's games, primarily because of her husband's tendency to argue with fans who were taunting and criticizing Orlando. "He would hear a fan yell at him," Carmen explained to Cope, "and he would put down his bat and turn around and find out who was yelling and then shake his finger at him."

Although Cepeda's play impressed his mother—and many other spectators, for that matter—some members of the Giants' organization didn't think he could play in the major leagues. They didn't feel Cepeda deserved an invitation to spring training. In their minds, he was not a prospect.

Pedrín Zorrilla and Alex Pómpez did not share that opinion. As the two men who had discovered Cepeda for the Giants, they knew about his talent. They pleaded with Giants' owner Horace Stoneham to invite Cepeda to spring training. They felt he deserved a legitimate chance to make the team.

The glowing reports put forth by Pómpez and Zorrilla convinced Stoneham not to trade Cepeda to the Cleveland Indians, who badly wanted to make a deal for "The Baby Bull." Stoneham believed that Cepeda should be brought to spring training with the Giants, who had just announced their move from New York to San Francisco. In fact, Stoneham came away so impressed that he made a bold prediction to *The Sporting News* about the upcoming 1958 season. "Orlando Cepeda will open the season at first base," Stoneham told sportswriter Bob Stevens, "for us in San Francisco."

# Chapter Three

# Home of the Giants

Horace Stoneham had already made up his mind that he wanted to see Cepeda play every day for his team in 1958. With the Giants having relocated from the East Coast to the West Coast, Stoneham wanted new players and a new identity for the team. But San Francisco manager Bill Rigney still had to be convinced about Cepeda. After all, Rigney had several contenders for the Giants' first base position. The group included veteran Whitey Lockman, who was near retirement, and a top minor league prospect named Willie McCovey.

Orlando reported to the Giants' spring training base in Phoenix, Arizona. Looking a bit clumsy in his baggy new uniform, Cepeda worked out with a team that featured an array of talented young players, along with several veteran stars. The group of established all-stars included center fielder Willie the "Say Hey Kid" Mays, one of the greatest all-around players in the game, and Dominican right-hander Juan Marichal, perhaps the greatest Latin American pitcher ever.

Marichal and Mays were proven players; Cepeda was not. Although *The Sporting News* had labeled him the best rookie prospect in the National League, he had never played a game above class Triple-A. Still only twenty, he had plenty to learn about the subtleties of playing major league baseball.

Cepeda's chances of winning the first base job had improved a bit, what with the power-hitting Bill White still serving in the U.S. Army. White, the Giants' starting first baseman two years earlier, had missed all of the 1957 season while in the military. White's continuing absence left Cepeda, Whitey Lockman, and Willie McCovey as the frontrunners for the position. Cepeda and McCovey had the most talent, but Lockman had experience and knowledge on his side.

Cepeda understood that he could use some advice from Lockman, one of the team's longtime veterans. Throughout spring training, Lockman taught Cepeda what he knew about playing first base. Bill Rigney asked Lockman to keep a close eye on Cepeda and keep him updated on the youngster's progress.

Several days later, Rigney asked Lockman about Cepeda. Lockman replied that the rookie was a "year away." Rigney thought out loud, "A year away from what?" In baseball terminology, a "year away" is a phrase usually meant to describe young players who need more training in the minor leagues. In other words, according to Lockman's words, Cepeda might not be ready to play for the Giants until next season. So who would play first base in 1958? And what would Rigney tell his boss, Horace Stoneham, who wanted to see Cepeda playing for the Giants *right now?*

After a brief pause, Lockman clarified his "year away" comment to Rigney. He said that Cepeda was "a year away from the Hall of Fame." Rigney smiled, realizing that Lockman had been making a play on words. The manager didn't have to wonder about first base anymore. He also didn't have to worry about what he would say to Horace Stoneham. The owner's choice, Orlando Cepeda, would be the Giants' first baseman on Opening Day.

Others shared the opinions held by Stoneham and Lockman. Frank Lane, the general manager of the Cleveland Indians, called Cepeda the best young player he'd seen in years. Lane had seen Cepeda torment his Indians during spring training, going 3-for-4 with four RBIs in his debut.

On April 15, the Giants started the regular season in front of a packed crowd at Seals Stadium, their new home ballpark. With the first pitch just five minutes away, Orlando finally signed his first major league contract. It would pay him the grand sum of $7,000. Coming from such a poor upbringing in Puerto Rico, it seemed like a king's ransom.

Playing in his first major league game, Orlando had the misfortune of facing the undisputed ace of the Los Angeles Dodgers. He was hard-throwing right-hander Don Drysdale, who had earned a reputation as one of the game's most intimidating pitchers. He liked to throw pitches toward the inside part of home plate, often knocking down batters who stood too close to the plate. Drysdale was especially tough on right-handed hitters, thanks to a tricky side-arming motion that hid the ball from the batter's view.

Given Drysdale's reputation and Cepeda's lack of experience, no one would have been surprised if Orlando struck out three or four times in his major league debut. Taking his first major league at-bat against one of the game's most feared pitchers, Orlando grounded into a double play. It was a tough way to start his career in the big leagues.

Fortunately for Cepeda, Drysdale lasted only three and two-thirds innings that day. So when Cepeda came to bat for the second time in the game, he faced reliever Don "The Weasel" Bessent instead. Although he was also a right-handed thrower, "The Weasel" wasn't nearly as tough on right-handed batters as Drysdale. He also didn't throw as hard as Drysdale. After working the count to three balls and one strike, Cepeda went smartly with one of Bessent's change-ups and drove a ball on the fly toward right-center field. The ball carried, and carried some more, clearing the right field fence at Seals Stadium for a 390-foot home run. In the long history of professional baseball, only a handful of players had managed to hit home runs in their first major league games. Cepeda had just joined that elite group.

The opposite field home run, which helped the Giants post an 8-0 win against their rivals, made him an instant hit with the hometown fans. It was also a sign of good things to come. Cepeda continued to hit well during the early weeks of the season. Giants' farm director Carl Hubbell, a onetime pitching great and Hall of Famer, called him the best young player he'd seen since Willie Mays came to the majors. "And in some respects he might even top the 'Say Hey Kid,'" Hubbell added in his conversation with *The Sporting News*. Others in the organization joined in the chorus heralding Cepeda. Bill Rigney called him the "best young right-hand-ed power hitter" he'd ever seen. Although such praises were well-intentioned, they sometimes raised expectations to an unfair level. Hubbell and Rigney probably didn't mean to do it, but they had just placed some additional and unneeded pressure on their rookie slugger.

Fortunately, the pressure didn't bother Orlando during his first summer in the major leagues. He remained confi-dent. "I see no pitch yet I cannot hit," he told reporters over and over. No pitch seemed to faze him, whether it be a fast-ball, curve-ball or slider. "He is annoying every pitcher in the league," Willie Mays told Jack Orr of *Sport Magazine*. "He is strong, he hits to all fields . . . He's the most relaxed first-year man I ever saw." Cepeda hit for both power and aver-age throughout the summer, helping the Giants stay in the pennant race until the final days of the season. If not for their sub-.500 play in August and September, the Giants might have finished even higher than their surprising third-place tally.

Like most rookies, Orlando also made his share of mis-takes. Most of his miscues seemed to come on the bases, when he tried to take an extra base. He had good speed, having been clocked the fastest of all the Giants in spring training, but didn't always seem to understand the limits of his running ability. At times, he didn't pay attention to his third base coach, who was warning him to stop. In one game, Cepeda foolishly tried to advance from first to third base on a ground ball, but was thrown out. Furious over the baserunning error, Bill Rigney yelled at Cepeda, criticizing him in front of the rest of the team. He even threatened to send the rookie first baseman back to the minor leagues. Rigney's angry reaction so upset Cepeda that he started to cry. Orlando even considered quitting the team and going home. After he had some time to think, he reconsidered and stayed with the Giants. He hit well in his next game, and kept on hitting.

Orlando finished his first big league season with 96 RBIs. He also batted .312, the seventh-highest figure in the National League. He stole 15 bases, surprising those who expected such a big man to be a slow runner. Accomplishments like those made him popular with the fans, who voted him the Giants' "Most Valuable Player."

Cepeda's popularity with the fans was startling. In fact, he seemed more popular in San Francisco than Willie Mays, the team's best player. There were several reasons that explained the fans' loyalties. For one, Mays had become a star during his years in New York, prior to the team's move to the West Coast. In the meantime, Orlando was San Francisco's star. And while Willie was a private person who preferred to keep to himself, Orlando seemed to enjoy talking to reporters, who in turn wrote favorable stories about him. He also liked to visit public places—like music and dance clubs—throughout San Francisco. "Right from the beginning, I fell in love with the city," Orlando told Ron Fimrite of *Sports Illustrated* in a 1991 interview. "On Thursdays, I would go to the 'Copacabana' to hear the Latin music. On Sundays, after games, I'd go to the 'Jazz Workshop' for the jam sessions." At places like these, Orlando met and talked to many people. Thanks to his outgoing personality and frequent smiles, he made many friends—quickly.

Unlike other players, Cepeda always seemed to be thinking about the people who attended San Francisco's games.
An incident during his rookie season typified his fan-friend-
ly nature. During a game at Seals Stadium, Cepeda chased
a pop fly into foul territory. He raced toward the railing that
kept fans in the stands and out of the field of play. As he
neared the railing, a fan reached out with his hand and
caught the ball. Several ballpark security men surrounded
the fan, wanting to eject him from the ballpark for interfer-
ing with a ball that might have been in play. The security
guards were about to do so when they heard a voice yelling
in their direction. "No, no, no," shouted Cepeda, who felt
the fan was simply doing the natural thing by trying to catch
the ball. Orlando pleaded with the security guards not to
eject the fan, who was finally allowed to remain in his seat.

Cepeda also impressed the baseball writers who voted on
the National League's post-season awards. They unani-
mously selected him as the league's Rookie of the Year, the
top first-year player. It seemed *The Sporting News* had been
justified in calling Cepeda the top rookie prospect in the
National League prior to the season.

Offering his reaction to the news, Cepeda hoped the
"Rookie of the Year" award would send a favorable message
to youngsters in his native Puerto Rico. "I hope my good for-
tune," Cepeda told United Press International, "will encourage my fellow Puerto Ricans to try to excel in sports—particularly baseball." With players like Cepeda and Roberto
Clemente already in the major leagues, the Puerto Rican pop-
ulation certainly had two positive role models to draw from.

Yet, Cepeda's rookie season did not come and go without
some rocky moments. He made his share of mistakes, sometimes running through his coach's signs and getting thrown
out trying to take an extra base. Cepeda was also involved in
an unfortunate incident. During a game against the Pirates,
Giants' right-hander Rubén Gómez (one of Cepeda's close

friends) threw a pitch that nailed Pittsburgh's Bill Mazeroski. Later in the game, Pirate pitcher Vernon Law threw an inside pitch that almost hit Gómez, who fell to the ground. The home plate umpire warned Law about intentionally throwing at opposing hitters. Pirate manager Danny Murtaugh then came out to protest. He felt that Gómez should have been thrown out for hitting Mazeroski earlier in the game. As Murtaugh argued, players from the Pirates and Giants streamed onto the field and soon started brawling. Angry with Murtaugh and eager to support Gómez, Cepeda started to make a move for one of the bats in the Giants' dugout. Luckily, Willie Mays put his arms around Cepeda and prevented "The Baby Bull" from picking up the dangerous wooden weapon. Nonetheless, the National League punished Cepeda by giving him a $100 fine.

Cepeda and Gómez became involved in another incident during the 1958–59 Winter League season. The two friends were teammates once again, this time with the Santurce Crabbers. In the fifth game of a tightly fought playoff series, Gómez hit Mayaguez outfielder Joe Christopher on the head with one of his pitches. Although the "beanball" forced Christopher to leave the game, his protective helmet prevented any serious injury. The Mayaguez fans, however, were not happy with Gómez. They booed him every time he came to the plate. Some of the rowdier fans even threw fruit onto the field.

The fans then became upset with Cepeda when he argued a call at first base. Some of the angrier spectators demanded that the umpires throw Cepeda out of the game, but they allowed him to remain.

In the eighth inning, a Mayaguez batter hit a foul pop-up to the right of the first base bag. Cepeda ran over to try to make a catch, but found himself dodging an array of apples, oranges, and beer bottles being thrown from the stands. As a result, he missed the pop-up. One of the oranges hit Cepeda in the face. A bottle hit him in the chest. Orlando also heard one of the fans shout an insult about his deceased father. Angry with the fans because of their nasty words and actions, Cepeda picked up the foul ball and fired it toward the stands. Fortunately, the ball hit a railing and bounced back toward the playing field. Still, the fans became even angrier with Cepeda and began throwing more bottles and pieces of fruit onto the field. The umpires finally decided to forfeit the game.

As Cepeda and Gómez tried to exit the stadium, they found thousands of fans waiting for them. Some of them had machetes (a kind of knife) in their hands. The two ballplayers finally managed to leave the ballpark—with a police escort.

The fans had reacted badly, but Cepeda was not blameless, either. The league fined him $200 for throwing the baseball toward the stands. Worse yet, Orlando was charged with criminal assault. Santurce owner Pedrín Zorrilla put up $500 bail to get him released from jail. Later on, the charges against Cepeda would be dropped. Unfortunately, the incident wouldn't be Orlando's last brush with the law.

## Chapter Four

# The Second Season

In spite of his problems with the fans in Mayaguez, Cepeda enjoyed his winter in Puerto Rico. He batted nearly .400 for Santurce. In one game, he hit a home run, a triple, and two doubles to lead Santurce to victory. Some of the fans responded by calling him "Perucho." After years of *negative* comparisons to his father, Orlando had finally gained favor with the hometown fans in Puerto Rico.

Even more importantly, Orlando made one of the most important commitments of his life. On January 9, 1959, he announced his engagement to Ana Hilda Piño, a shy girl who attended school in the nearby Barrio Obrero. The couple would marry in 1960 and would eventually move into a nice house in Santa Rosa, a suburb of San Juan.

Orlando's personal life was going well, as was his baseball life. When the Giants decided to trade away Bill White, one of his competitors for the first base job, his feelings of security with the team improved even more. Over the winter, there had been talk that the Giants might move Cepeda to third base to make room for White at first. The Giants put a stop to that rumor when they dealt White to the St. Louis Cardinals. By trading White, the Giants had given Cepeda a complete vote of confidence in his ability to handle the first base job.

Cepeda did not feel as good about his salary, however. As the National League's Rookie of the Year, Cepeda felt he deserved a sizeable raise. He wanted to be paid $20,000 for the 1959 season. He asked his brother, Pedro, to serve as his unofficial agent, but the Giants refused to give in to the Cepedas' asking price. Orlando eventually settled for a salary of $17,000.

Cepeda started out his second season by collecting hits in nine consecutive games. He banged out 15 hits in his first 39 at-bats before experiencing a brief slump, as National League pitchers learned to exploit some of his weaknesses at the plate. Hitting with little power, and with his batting average a mediocre .267, Cepeda went to the bench for a brief time. He didn't start for three consecutive games.

On May 16, Orlando returned to the starting lineup. Almost immediately, The Baby Bull looked like the player the Giants had seen in 1958. He hammered a home run and a single in four at-bats, driving in four runs to lead San Francisco to a 9-2 thumping of Cincinnati. And that was just the start. Cepeda collected hits in fifteen of eighteen games, compiling a batting average of .427. He also drove in 23 runs. On June 4, Cepeda enjoyed his biggest game of the season. Playing at Milwaukee's County Stadium, he hit his 11th and 12th home runs and drove in a whopping seven runs. His second home run traveled an estimated 500 feet—a remarkable distance. The explosion helped the Giants come from behind to defeat the Milwaukee Braves, 11-5. With the win, San Francisco improved to within two and a half games of the first-place Braves.

On June 19, Cepeda helped the Giants move into first place with a dramatic 10th-inning comeback against the Braves. Cepeda picked up a single during the two-run rally and then scored the game-winning run. Unfortunately, San Francisco's newfound ownership of first place didn't last long, as the Giants lost to Milwaukee the next day, 4-1. The Braves also won the following game to increase their lead to a game and a half. The Giants wouldn't return to the National League's top spot until just after the All-Star break, when Cepeda singled and stole a base in a 3-2 win over Cincinnati.

Although Orlando was playing and hitting extremely well, the Giants faced a dilemma at his first base position. One of their top prospects, a young slugger named Willie McCovey, was having a phenomenal season in the minor leagues. Ironically, the Giants had signed McCovey on the very same day they had signed Cepeda in 1955. Four years later, McCovey was now ready to move up to the major leagues. Unfortunately, he couldn't play any position but first base. That position, of course, belonged to Cepeda.

On July 30, the Giants recalled McCovey from their top farm team. Manager Bill Rigney asked Cepeda to move back to his original position of third base. Hoping that it would help the team, Orlando agreed to the move. He played the "hot corner" for four games, but made three errors and several other mistakes. In one game, he overthrew McCovey so badly that the ball ended up hitting a woman who was sitting in the stands behind first base. Cepeda's fielding proved so poor at third base that the Giants moved him to left field. That also proved to be too much of a challenge for the young Cepeda. "I just wasn't ready mentally," Orlando told *Sports Illustrated* in 1991. "I know I could've played left field if I put my mind to it, but I was only twenty-one years old and very sensitive. Friends . . . kept telling me I should demand to play first [base]. It was all pride with me. And ignorance." With Cepeda feeling uncomfortable in the outfield, Rigney finally decided to put him back at first base. He would remain there for the rest of the season.

For most of July and August, the Giants held on to first place. In late August, they built up their biggest lead to four and a half games. But then the Giants lost six of their next eight games. In late September, they lost three straight games to the Dodgers and fell from first place to third place. After having picked up so many clutch hits throughout the season, Cepeda went only 2-for-13 in that critical series.

Cepeda bounced back quickly by driving in key runs in four of the next five games, but San Francisco lost four of the contests. Unbelievably, the Giants wound up losing the pennant to the Dodgers by four full games and settling for third place behind Milwaukee. It was a bitter end to what had been a fun summer.

Orlando Cepeda's first pennant race had concluded with a series of heartbreaking losses. Yet, he had learned a lot during the late-season race. Except for those games against the Dodgers, he had proven to himself that he could hit very well in games that carried enormous pressure. The experience, although a losing one, would help Cepeda again and again during his career.

Although Orlando did not like to lose, he handled defeats much better than his father had. He tried not to dwell on losses. "If I stay mad, I get ulcers," Cepeda told *Sport Magazine*. "So I leave everything at the ballpark."

Yet, Orlando still owned intense pride in wanting to play the game well. He felt bad when he made mistakes in the field. Playing in a 1959 Winter League game for the Santurce Crabbers, Cepeda dropped a pop fly in the late innings. When the Crabbers trotted into the dugout at the end of the inning, Santurce pitcher Juan Pizarro made a joke about Cepeda's misplay. Although Pizarro meant no harm, Orlando didn't take it well. He lashed back at the veteran pitcher. Santurce manager Luis Olmo, seemingly siding with Pizarro, chipped in with his own sarcastic comment about Cepeda's error. That only made Orlando more upset. "If you are not satisfied with my play," Cepeda shouted toward his manager, "I will quit." When Olmo refused to give his star a vote of confidence, Orlando did what he said he would—he left the team. It seemed like an overreaction, but it showed that he took his performance very seriously. If he felt that his manager was dissatisfied with his play, Orlando did not want to continue to play for that team.

# Chapter Five

# Trouble with the Boss

In the middle of a disappointing 1960 season, the Giants decided to fire Bill Rigney as manager. The Giants had a winning record after their first fifty-eight games, but the front office considered the team an underachieving lot and decided to make Rigney the fall guy. They replaced him on an interim basis with Tom Sheehan, a team scout whom Cepeda liked. Sheehan would manage the Giants for the rest of 1960 and then return to his position as a scout.

Although some observers believed the Giants had played below their potential during the first half of the 1960 season, Rigney and Cepeda appeared to get along well. They had rarely argued in front of others. In the spring of 1961, that apparent harmony came to an end.

In early March, sportswriter Dick Young of the *New York Daily News* interviewed Rigney, the ex-manager, for an article he was writing about the Giants. According to Young, Rigney complained that the Giants would never win the pennant until some of their key players "grew up." First and foremost at the top of the list was Orlando Cepeda. "Winning the pennant isn't as important to him as it should be," Young quoted Rigney as saying. "That's one thing he still must learn."

Rigney's words angered Cepeda, a sensitive man who did not like to be criticized in public. The young first baseman delivered some uncomplimentary words of his own in describing his manager. "That man lost the pennant for us,"

Cepeda yelled to a reporter from the Associated Press. "He has no guts. He can't manage at all. He doesn't know baseball or ballplayers."

Orlando wasn't done. He criticized Rigney for playing him out of position at third base, despite the fact that he was an accomplished fielder at first base. He went on to say that Rigney constantly picked on him and blamed him for things that were not his fault. He said that Rigney called him a troublemaker. He accused Rigney of talking about him behind his back.

For his part, Rigney claimed he had been misquoted in the article by Dick Young. The manager said he had never accused Cepeda of not wanting to win. Rigney also denied ever calling Cepeda a troublemaker.

"Rigney was awfully nice to me in 1958," Cepeda told Charles Einstein of *Sport Magazine*. "But I don't know what happened after that. Last year in the clubhouse in front of everybody, he said to me, 'You may be a big man in Puerto Rico, but not here.' Why would he say something like that to me? And especially in front of everybody."

After a while, Cepeda's bad feelings about Rigney cooled off. Several years later, a writer asked Cepeda to name the greatest manager he had played for during his career. "Bill Rigney," Orlando answered without hesitation. In fact, Cepeda went on to call Rigney a "great man," and thanked him for showing such confidence in his ability when he first came up to the big leagues.

His current feelings for Rigney put aside, Cepeda proceeded to put together the finest year of his young career. Playing for a new manager in Alvin Dark, he willingly went to the outfield to start the season and worked hard at improving his fielding. When he returned to the infield, he fielded beautifully at first base, making only two errors on the season. More importantly, Cepeda's offensive game continued to grow. He led the team in hitting with a .311 mark.

He led the entire National League with 46 home runs *and* 142 RBIs. At times carrying the Giants' offense on his back, Cepeda helped his club become a contender in the National League pennant race. The Giants finished a respectable 85-69, good for third place behind the Cincinnati Reds and Los Angeles Dodgers.

A doubleheader that the Giants played on the Fourth of July showed what Cepeda was capable of doing when he was performing at his best. Playing both games against the Chicago Cubs, Cepeda rapped out seven hits in nine at-bats. His hitting in the first game was particularly impressive. He feasted on Chicago's pitching staff by going 5-for-5 and driving in eight runs. His offensive rampage included an incredibly long home run against Jim Brewer, a tough reliever. It was one of the most memorable blasts of Cepeda's career.

Even though the Giants fell short of winning the pennant that year, some followers of the team felt Cepeda deserved to win the National League's Most Valuable Player award. He had been that good—the league's most feared hitter in 1961. The MVP, however, was an award that usually went to a player from the team that finished in first place.

Still, the results of the voting disappointed Cepeda and his fans when they heard the MVP announcement in November. Even though he had led the league in two of the most important offensive categories, and finished second to Los Angeles' Gil Hodges in fielding percentage among first basemen, he didn't come close to capturing the award. The winner, Frank Robinson of the pennant-winning Reds, picked up 219 total points. Cepeda finished a distant second, with only 117 points. Robinson might have deserved to win the MVP, but it seemed like Cepeda should have gotten a little bit better support. "What was bad about it was that Orlando was so far behind in the voting—100 points behind Robinson," complained scout and owner Pedrín Zorrilla, who made his comments during an interview with Myron Cope of

*Sport Magazine.* "Orlando's pride was hurt and so were the prides of his countrymen."

As Cepeda wondered what he had to do to win over the writers, he continued his season in the Puerto Rican Winter League. He was a full-fledged star, not only in the United States but in his native land. His growing stardom gained him a powerful influence among the Puerto Rican fans, as an incident during a game between Santurce and Arecibo soon proved.

Arecibo fans had gained a reputation as some of the loudest and wildest in the Puerto Rican League. When the second base umpire made a questionable call that went in favor of Santurce, the Arecibo fans erupted with a series of boos and catcalls. They continued to show their disgust with the umpire for the remainder of the night. After the game, a large group of fans crowded against a fence that bordered the playing field. The umpires usually walked through a gate in the fence in order to get to their dressing room. The gathering of angry fans near the gate seemed to create the potential for a violent episode.

That's when Cepeda stepped in. "Orlando went over there and spoke to the crowd in Spanish," umpire Paul Pryor told *Sport Magazine.* "He told them, 'The umpire was closer to the play than you were, and even if he made a mistake, he is only human.' They stopped booing and went home." The reaction of the Arecibo fans was even more remarkable considering that Cepeda played for Santurce—the enemy team.

As the 1962 season approached, expectations for Cepeda continued to grow. One sportswriter, Murray Robinson of the *New York Journal-American,* hinted that Cepeda might surpass Roger Maris's single-season total of 61 home runs. Maris himself had just broken Babe Ruth's record of 60 home runs, a mark that had stood since 1927. And why did Robinson think that Cepeda could rebreak the record so quickly? First, the National League had decided to add two expansion clubs, with each likely to have weak pitching staffs prone to giving up the longball. Second, all National League teams would now be playing 162 games—instead of 154. With eight extra games on the schedule, Cepeda might be able to add four or five home runs to his total.

Those expectations would turn out to be a little high, but both Cepeda and the Giants played like champions during the first month of the season. With Cepeda and Willie Mays hitting the ball incredibly hard, the Giants won their first five games. Toward the end of April, they began forging a ten-game winning streak. Cepeda and Mays played so well that some writers already called them the two main contenders for the National League's MVP award.

According to United Press International, Cepeda and Mays had a strong personal rivalry going between them. In other words, each player wanted to outdo the other. Given the sometimes tense feelings between Cepeda and Mays, that was no surprise. Yet, their rivalry didn't hurt the team. By the end of May, Cepeda was hitting .352; Mays was batting in the low .300s. With Cepeda and Mays anchoring the middle of the lineup, the Giants won forty of their first fifty-five games. They held first place for nearly six weeks.

The Giants them slumped in June and July. They rebounded a bit, before hitting another dry spell in mid-August. With the season in jeopardy of falling apart, the Giants opened up an important three-game series against the Philadelphia Phillies. Cepeda proceeded to rap nine hits in 13 at-bats. His offensive barrage included four home runs and eight RBIs. Carrying the Giants on his back, Cepeda led the team to three straight wins over the Phillies. The Giants, who had almost given up hope of catching the Dodgers in the standings, felt like contenders once again.

By September, Cepeda's hitting had tailed off. Manager Alvin Dark could live with that, but he couldn't live with Orlando's lack of effort during a game against the Milwaukee Braves. Appearing as a pinch-hitter with two outs in the ninth inning, Cepeda hit a ground ball but didn't run hard to first base. Why? He was upset that Dark had benched him from the starting lineup, after hitting well the previous night. Dark fined Cepeda for not hustling. Although Orlando may have had reason to be upset with Dark, he had no excuse for not running hard. It was one of the most shameful moments of Cepeda's proud career.

On September 12, the Dodgers and Giants owned nearly identical records, with Los Angeles just a half-game better in the standings. Opening up a key road trip, the Giants lost two straight games in Cincinnati. They then lost four straight games to the Pittsburgh Pirates. In the meantime, the Dodgers built up a seven-game winning streak. With only thirteen games left on the schedule, Los Angeles enjoyed a four-game lead. The Giants' chances of coming back seemed remote, especially with a tired Cepeda struggling through a late-season slump.

San Francisco won only six of its next twelve games, but got lucky when Los Angeles ran into a slump. The Dodgers picked up only three victories against nine losses during the same time frame. As a result, the Dodgers held just a one-game lead on the Giants going into the final day of the season.

With the National League pennant on the line, manager Alvin Dark decided that Orlando Cepeda couldn't help the Giants in their last game. Dark felt his star first baseman was tired, exhausted from having played so many games during the regular season after another year of winter ball. As a result, Dark benched Cepeda, the same player who had batted over .300 and belted 35 home runs for him during the season.

Disappointed that he did not get the chance to contribute to his team's most important game, Orlando sat down and cried. "That was the worst day of my life," he told Stan Isaacs of *Newsday.*

It wasn't a very good day for teammate Felipe Alou, either. The Giants' regular right fielder also sat out the game—the result of another one of Dark's controversial decisions. Fortunately, the day did not turn out to be a loss for the Giants as a team. Willie Mays hit a dramatic home run in the bottom of the eighth inning to give the Giants a critical 2-1 victory over the expansion Houston Colt .45s. The win put the Giants in a tie with the Dodgers, who had lost their game to the St. Louis Cardinals. As upset as Orlando was about missing the game against Houston, he realized he would get another chance to play. Cepeda was about to participate in his first-ever tiebreaking play-off series.

Rather than play a single game to break the tie, National League rules called for a best two-out-of-three series to determine the winner of the pennant. With the first game scheduled for San Francisco's Candlestick Park, Alvin Dark returned Cepeda to the starting lineup. He would play first base and bat fifth against the Dodgers' phenomenal left-hander, Sandy Koufax.

The Giants opened up an early 3-0 lead against Koufax, who looked tired on the mound and left after one inning. In the bottom of the sixth inning, Mays and Cepeda hit back-to-back home runs to put the game away. San Francisco coasted to an 8-0 win.

Cepeda's bat fell quiet in the second game, which was played at Los Angeles' Dodger Stadium. Facing tough right-hander Don Drysdale and the Dodger bullpen, Cepeda went 1-for-5. The Giants coughed up a five-run lead, allowing the Dodgers to score seven runs in the sixth and the game-winning run in the ninth. The loss by the Giants tied the series at a game apiece, forcing a decisive third game to be played at Dodger Stadium.

In this game, the Giants opened up a 2-0 lead, but the Dodgers bounced back with four runs in the middle innings. As the game headed to the top of the ninth, the Dodgers held a 4-2 lead. Given the strength of Los Angeles' pitching, it didn't seem too likely that San Francisco would be able to score one run, much less two runs to tie the game. The Giants' season seemed to be coming to an end.

Yet, there were still three outs to be recorded. Mateo "Matty" Alou, a slap hitter from the Dominican Republic, led off the inning with a pinch-hit single. With one out, Willie McCovey and Felipe Alou—Matty's brother—each drew walks, loading the bases. Willie Mays followed by hitting a ferocious line drive up the middle, off the hand of relief pitcher Ed Roebuck. The infield hit brought home one run and knocked Roebuck from the game.

Dodger manager Walter Alston called on Stan Williams, a hard-throwing right-hander who liked to throw inside pitches. He also liked to hit opposing batters with pitches if they stood too close to the plate. Most National League scouts considered Williams one of the toughest pitchers—and perhaps the meanest—in the major leagues.

With the bases still loaded, Cepeda offered at Williams' first pitch. It was a rising fastball—a tough pitch—that Cepeda swung at and missed. Orlando was now in the hole at 0-and-1. He needed to be ready for the next pitch.

Cepeda went with Williams' second delivery, driving the ball deep toward right field. Frank "Hondo" Howard, the Dodgers' six-foot, nine-inch giant in the outfield, made a nice, reaching stab of the drive, but it was deep enough to score pinch-runner Ernie Bowman from third base. The most important sacrifice fly of Cepeda's career had tied the game at 4-4.

The Giants then took the lead, scoring two more runs on a pair of walks and an error. Billy Pierce came on to retire the Dodgers in order in the bottom of the ninth, sealing an incredible 6-4 win *and* the pennant for the Giants. Thanks in no small part to Orlando Cepeda, the Giants were headed to the World Series for the first time since their world championship year of 1954.

A huge crowd of 75,000 fans waited for the arrival of the Giants' plane at the airport in San Francisco. Some of the fans even streamed onto the runway, forcing the pilot to think about landing at another airport! Thankfully, airport officials successfully cleared the runway, allowing the team plane to land as scheduled.

Unfortunately, Orlando's regular-season struggles continued in the World Series. Through the first four games against the New York Yankees, he went 0-for-12. He didn't even get a chance to swing the bat in Game Two, having been benched by Alvin Dark. Now, with the Series even at two games apiece, he was sitting out Game Five. What was causing his continuing problems at the plate? The Giants sent him to a doctor to find out. "He examined my heart, everything," Cepeda told Stan Isaacs of *Newsday*. "He told me I've played too many baseball games."

The previous winter, Cepeda had played 100 games in the Puerto Rican Winter League. It was the fifth consecutive year he had played for the Giants during the summer and for his native Puerto Rico during the winter months. Enough was enough. Orlando needed a rest.

With Cepeda glued to the dugout bench, the Giants lost the fifth game. A 5-3 defeat put San Francisco one game away from elimination. Would Alvin Dark allow Cepeda to play, or he would he keep him out of the lineup one more day? It might be the Giants' last game of the season.

Dark felt he needed Cepeda, tired or not, to give the Giants their best chance against the Yankees. So Orlando returned to the starting lineup for Game Six. The day off seemed to refresh Cepeda, who felt strong enough to use a heavier bat. In the second inning, Orlando hit a routine ground ball to Tony Kubek at shortstop. Without warning, the ball took a bad hop, jumping over Kubek's head into left field for a single. The fortunate base hit seemed to relax Cepeda. In his second at-bat against Yankee ace Whitey Ford, Orlando launched a double into the right-center field gap, scoring Willie Mays. A base hit by Jim Davenport then scored Cepeda, giving the Giants the winning run in a 5-2 victory over the Yankees. Cepeda wasn't done, adding another RBI single in the fifth inning to cap off a 3-for-4 performance.

Orlando's heroics earned him another start at first base in the seventh and final game. Unfortunately, Cepeda could not duplicate his hitting brilliance of Game Six. He went 0-for-3 against Yankee right-hander Ralph Terry. None of the other Giants' hitters did much against Terry, either. Only Willie McCovey and pitcher Jack Sanford hit safely through the first eight innings.

In the ninth inning, the Giants tried to rally from a 1-0 deficit. With two outs and Matty Alou on first base, Willie Mays lined a pitch toward right center field. At first, the ball looked like it would roll to the wall, which would allow Alou to score the tying run all the way from first. But Yankee rightfielder Roger Maris cut the ball off in the gap so quickly that the speedy Alou had to stop at third base. In the meantime, Mays steamed into second base. He now represented the potential game-winning run.

The dangerous McCovey stepped to the plate, with Cepeda waiting in the on-deck circle. Some of the sportswriters attending the game thought the Yankees would intentionally walk McCovey to pitch to Cepeda. That way, the right-handed Terry would have the advantage of pitching against the right-handed Cepeda.

Yankee manager Ralph Houk surprised everyone by allowing Terry to pitch to the left-handed McCovey. As Cepeda remained planted to the on-deck circle, the sportswriters continued to question Houk's decision. Moments later, his strategy seemed doomed to failure. McCovey smacked a screaming line drive that appeared headed toward right-center field. If it reached the outfield, it would score both runners and give the Giants the world championship. It didn't. Yankee second baseman Bobby Richardson, well positioned on the right side of the infield, moved a step to his left and caught the line drive in his glove. The ball was hit so hard that Richardson fell to the ground, overpowered by the force of the drive. But he held on, giving the Yankees the title and capping off a heartbreaking defeat for the Giants. Cepeda never got to leave the on-deck circle for one more crack against the Yankee pitching staff.

Cepeda finished the Series with only three hits in 19 at-bats—for a poor .158 batting average. Several of the Giants' best hitters, including Willie Mays and Willie McCovey, also struggled against the Yankees, but Cepeda seemed to draw most of the attention from the San Francisco media. Several writers criticized Cepeda for failing to hit in the clutch. His lack of timely hitting in the Series would have been easier to take if the Giants had managed to pull out a win in the final game. Unfortunately, Orlando's first World Series had resulted in a double defeat—both for himself and his team. It was a disappointing way to finish what had been an otherwise terrific season.

# Chapter Six

# A Clubhouse Divided

The new season did not begin well. Unlike most of the other starters on the Giants, Cepeda was not offered a pay raise. In fact, he was told to take a pay*cut* for the 1963 season. The Giants wanted to pay him $4,000 less than what he made in 1962. Orlando hated that idea so much that he elected not to report to spring training on time.

As the Giants held spring training in Arizona, Cepeda grew even angrier when he read a newspaper story that quoted his manager, Alvin Dark. At a press conference held by the Giants' skipper, Dark informed reporters about the results of a plus-minus system he had used in 1961 and 1962. Dark gave a player a plus each time he did something good and a minus for each mistake he made. He then added up the totals to see what each player's final "grade" came out to be.

Under Dark's system, Willie Mays led all of the Giants with 100 points during the 1962 season. That was no surprise, considering that most people considered the "Say Hey Kid" the team's best player and Cepeda the second-best player. Cepeda's grade came as quite a shock, however. According to Dark, Cepeda had come out with many more minuses than plusses, especially during the last month and a half of the season.

By 1963, Cepeda's problems with Alvin Dark had become common knowledge. Cepeda didn't like it when Dark ordered him not to play any more Latino music in the

clubhouse. More importantly, Cepeda resented Dark's decision to ban Latino players from speaking Spanish in the
clubhouse and on the team bus. "I said, 'This is ridicu-
lous,'" Cepeda recalled in an article that appeared in *Sport
Magazine*. "I'm proud of my language. I'm Spanish. This is
going to be the worst thing if we talk [in] English. Because
we can communicate better in Spanish." Most of the other
Latin players felt the same way.

Cepeda also felt that Dark blamed the black and Latino
players on the team whenever the Giants lost. He wondered
why the manager repeatedly pointed out the mistakes of
minority players like him, Willie Mays, and Willie McCovey.
That was a bit strange, considering that they were the best
players on the team.

Cepeda also resented Dark for segregating the clubhouse—putting the blacks in one section of the locker room,
the Latinos in another, and the whites in a third section.
This was not the way to foster team unity. And it was clearly an example of the kind of racism that recent civil rights
laws had been trying to eliminate.

Given the atmosphere in the clubhouse, the relationship
between Cepeda and Dark had become badly strained. During the 1962 World Series, a reporter had asked Cepeda if
Dark ever made special efforts to talk to him. "No," Cepeda
told Stan Isaacs of *Newsday*. "Sometimes you like somebody
to give you a pat on the back." Although Orlando insisted
that he had "nothing against" Dark, it was obvious that he
felt his manager didn't fully support him.

Dark's grading system gave Cepeda yet another reason to
feel hurt. Orlando had given the Giants his best effort in
1962 and had helped the team reach the World Series.
Although his statistics were not as impressive as they had
been in 1961, they were still good. Dark later called Cepeda to explain how his plus-minus system worked. He also

tried to assure Orlando that his season was not as bad as the many minuses indicated.

Orlando felt better after his telephone conversation with Dark. But he was still annoyed by the Giants' contract offer. "I want a raise and I'll sit at home until I get it," Cepeda told Jack McDonald of *The Sporting News.* The Giants eventually agreed to give Orlando a $1,000 boost in pay. It wasn't much, but it was better than a paycut. With his new contract in hand, Cepeda reported to spring training in Phoenix, Arizona.

Cepeda had overcome one negative obstacle; another one came his way after the regular season began. On May 21, *Look* magazine published an article that made Cepeda angry. The article accused Orlando of having several faults, both as a player and as a person. *He doesn't hit well in the clutch. He is not a team player. He blames everyone else for his own problems. He holds out from signing his contract every year and reports late to spring training.* The article, written by *Look* sports editor Tim Cohane, blamed Cepeda for the Giants' inability to win the World Series in 1962. The article also made it seem that Cepeda was jealous of his teammate, Willie Mays.

Critics of Cepeda pointed to a game in 1962, when the Giants had visited the expansion New York Mets for the first time. During pregame introductions, the large crowd at Shea Stadium gave Mays a standing ovation; many of those New York fans had cheered for Mays in the 1950s, when Willie played for the New York Giants. According to some observers at Shea Stadium, Cepeda's body language during the ovation seemed to show jealousy on his part.

The accusations of jealousy really bothered Cepeda. Although he didn't really get along with Mays, and almost never socialized with him away from the ballpark, he insisted that jealousy was never an issue in his attitude toward the Giants' superstar. "Why would I be jealous of Willie?"

Cepeda said to Bob Stevens, correspondent for *The Sporting News*. "I'm proud to play on the same team with so great a player." Other players on the Giants supported Cepeda on this point. In an article in *Sport Magazine*, Willie McCovey said that all of the talk of Cepeda pouting and refusing to talk to Mays was "sheer nonsense."

The criticisms in the *Look* magazine feature so upset Cepeda that he decided to file a $1 million lawsuit against the publisher of the magazine. A United States District Court jury ruled against Cepeda, saying that there was no proof that Cohane had reported the story irresponsibly. In 1967, Cepeda and his lawyer appealed the decision to the U.S. Court of Appeals, but they lost their case the following year. About the only satisfaction that Cepeda received came when a judge ordered Cohane to spend ten days in jail for refusing to answer questions in federal court about the story. Cohane would not reveal the names of his sources, the ones that had criticized Cepeda.

Perhaps in response to all of the negative talk, the Giants began discussing the possibility of trading Cepeda. One newspaper report said the team had talked to the Pittsburgh Pirates about trading Cepeda for relief ace ElRoy "Roy" Face. Giants' owner Horace Stoneham denied the report and came to the defense of Cepeda. "I have no criticism whatever of Cepeda's play for us," Stoneham told Jack McDonald of *The Sporting News*, "and there is absolutely no truth to the claim he has been offered for trade."

And based on his on-field performance, why would the Giants want to trade Cepeda? As of May 20, his .318 batting average led the team. He had improved his average by cutting down on his swing with two strikes in the count. As a result, he was making more consistent contact with the ball. Orlando also felt stronger than he had in the past. "Every other winter, I had [played] too much baseball in Puerto Rico," said Orlando, who had decided not to play winter ball after the 1962 season. "This year I feel lots more zip. No more winter ball for Orlando," he told Jack McDonald of *The Sporting News.*

Boosted by the extra dose of strength, an energized Cepeda finished the season at .316, the second-highest batting average of his six years in the major leagues. Given Cepeda's contributions, the Giants couldn't realistically blame him for their failure to reach the World Series in 1963. It was mediocre pitching—and not the lack of hitting by Cepeda and the other team's top guns—that doomed the Giants to a third-place finish in the National League.

For a second straight winter, Orlando decided not to play winter ball. Instead, he lifted weights in the hope that he would become stronger and more durable. It was a plan that made sense.

One day, one of the weights fell off a barbell and hit the top of his right knee, the same knee he had injured as a youngster. The impact of the 80-pound weight damaged the knee again and caused him continuous pain. Orlando decided not to tell the Giants about it. He would keep playing without saying a word.

With his knee injury a secret, Orlando opted to make a big change in his preparation for the 1964 season. Even though he had batted for a high average in 1963, he wanted to become an even better hitter. He was still known as a slugger who pounded home runs and piled up RBIs for a living. Cepeda wanted to be known as a more well-rounded hitter. So he decided to change the kind of equipment he was using.

In the spring, Cepeda ordered his shipment of bats from the Hillerich and Bradsby Company in Louisville, Kentucky. Cepeda always needed a large supply because of his unusual superstition: he discarded each bat after he picked up a hit with it. Although he wasn't going to change the number of bats that he ordered, he was going to change the *size* of each bat. He asked Hillerich and Bradsby to make him 40-

ounce bats. No other major league player used a bat heavier than 39 ounces. Later in the season, Cepeda would switch to an even heavier model. He began using a 45-ounce bat. It was like swinging a tree trunk. Not even the great Babe Ruth had used such a large bat in regular season play.

Although the heavier bat made his swing a bit slower, it also made it more controlled. In the past, he was too far out in front, which resulted in weak foul pop-ups to the third baseman and catcher. With the bigger bat, Orlando could now get his body behind his swing and keep the ball fair while hitting it much harder. The slower swing also allowed him a little bit more time to watch each pitch.

As a result of the change, Cepeda enjoyed his fastest start as a Giant. He picked up six hits in his first nine at-bats, including a 3-for-4 outburst on Opening Day. It was a sign of great things to come, only to be interrupted by problems with his leg. He developed fluid on his knee, which forced him out of the lineup in late April through early May.

Some people around the Giants started to question whether Cepeda was really hurt. The skeptics included Cepeda's own manager, Alvin Dark, whom Orlando considered a prejudiced man. "Some people think that because we are Latins," Cepeda told Mark Mulvoy of *Sports Illustrated* several years later, "we are not supposed to get hurt. But my knee was hurt. Dark thought I was trying not to play. He treated me like a child. I am a human being, whether I am blue or black or white or green. We Latins are different, but we are still human beings. Dark did not respect our differences."

In spite of the trouble with his knee and the questions from his bosses, Orlando played some of the best ball of his career in 1964. In one early season game, he surprised the New York Mets by stealing home. The stolen base helped the Giants defeat the Mets by one run. And then in June, Cepeda went on a hitting rampage. On June 3, he hit a game-winning home run against the Pirates. Ten days later, he delivered a key double in the late innings that helped San Francisco defeat Milwaukee. On June 24, his first-inning home run gave the Giants a 2-1 win over the Reds. A few days later, he drove in the game-winning run in two consecutive games against the arch-rival Dodgers.

After the second win over the Dodgers, Alvin Dark praised Cepeda like never before. "Orlando has never been better," the manager told Bob Stevens of the *San Francisco Chronicle.* "His clutch performances have kept us in business."

With Cepeda leading the offense, the Giants remained in the "business" of the pennant race for most of the season. They stayed close to the Philadelphia Phillies, Cincinnati Reds, and St. Louis Cardinals, before eventually bowing out of the four-way chase on the second-to-last day of the season.

An army of injuries had prevented the Giants from overtaking first place. Key players like Cepeda, Willie McCovey, outfielders Jesus and Matty Alou, and pitching ace Juan Marichal all missed time because of one ailment or another. If the Giants had remained just a little bit healthier, they might have been able to hold out and win the National League title.

The Giants' fourth-place finish led to some changes. One of the biggest involved Cepeda's least favorite manager, Alvin Dark. The Giants fired Dark, replacing him with coach Herman Franks. After his fair share of problems with both Dark and Bill Rigney, Cepeda hoped for a better relationship with his third major league manager.

After the 1964 season, Cepeda returned to Puerto Rico to play in the Winter League. When his team ran out of catchers in one game, the team-oriented Orlando volunteered to go behind the plate. It turned out to be an unwise decision when his right knee locked. By aggravating his bad knee, Cepeda had no choice but to undergo an operation.

Cepeda should never have agreed to catch. The position required too much squatting and bending for someone who had a history of trouble with his knees. Orlando had allowed his sense of teamwork to go too far, at the expense of his own health and well-being.

The operation went well and Orlando reported to spring training. Unfortunately, Cepeda twisted his knee during the spring. He simply couldn't avoid problems with that area of his leg. "Whenever anything happens to me, it always seems to hit the same spot, the same knee," Cepeda complained to Arthur Daley of the *New York Times*.

There was actually a good reason why his right knee troubled him again and again. Orlando had been born with a malformed right leg, which was shorter than his left leg. In addition, he suffered from what longtime baseball writer Bob Broeg called "pancake-flat" feet. Since the bottoms of Cepeda's feet didn't have the normal arch of other people's feet, his knees had to absorb more of the shock whenever he ran.

Cepeda remembered the first time he had hurt his right knee as a major leaguer. "Back in 1961," Orlando told the *New York Times*, "I was sliding home when [Los Angeles Dodgers' catcher] John Roseboro blocked me off at the plate. My knee hit his shin guards and I was out for two or three days." A few weeks later, Cepeda's knee connected with the shin guard of St. Louis Cardinals' catcher Gene Oliver. The following year, Cepeda collided with Cleveland Indians' pitcher Gary Bell during a spring training game. In that incident, Bell's shoulder rammed into Cepeda's right knee. And then in 1964, Cepeda rounded third base and tried to stop quickly. As he did, he jammed his knee—again the right one.

In spite of the latest injury, Orlando tried to start the season on time. Yet, he had trouble running and hitting. On May 7, the Giants placed him on the disabled list. According to baseball rules, he would not be allowed to play for at least thirty days. As it turned out, he would be out of action for much longer than that.

After Orlando twisted his knee, he stopped doing the leg exercises that his doctor had told him to do. His leg became weak again. His right knee swelled. It caused him constant pain. The Giants sent Cepeda to the famed Mayo Clinic in Rochester, Minnesota. Doctors gave him an injection and told him to exercise by doing deep knee bends and some light running. But they didn't want him to play baseball just yet. He would have to wait until the knee became stronger.

Cepeda felt better, but the feeling didn't last. The swelling and the pain returned. As a result, he could not play. Yet, some people who followed the Giants doubted Cepeda. They accused him of "faking" an injury. Others called him a hypochondriac, someone who only imagined that he was hurt. Orlando heard the whispers. "I know they call me a fake," Cepeda told sportswriter Milton Gross of the *New York Post.* "I know they say that all this year I take money and give the team nothing for it. I know they say that I could play if I want to, but [that] I don't want to. The people who say that are ignorant." It was not the first time that a Latin American player had been criticized for not playing. It was not the first time that a minority player had been questioned about his injuries. All Cepeda had to do was ask another Puerto Rican and black star, Roberto Clemente of the Pirates. Some writers and fans had made a living out of calling Clemente a hypochondriac.

In mid-August, the Giants decided to bring Cepeda off the disabled list. It seemed like a strange decision, given that Orlando could not walk up and down the dugout stairs without limping. He could barely run at half of his usual speed. When George Vecsey of *Newsday* asked Herman Franks about Cepeda's return, the first-year manager snapped an angry reply. "Ask *him* about the knee," said

Franks, who seemed upset with his injured slugger. Just like Alvin Dark before him, Franks made it clear—in public— that he didn't care for Cepeda's attitude.

Although many people around the Giants continued to question Cepeda, he insisted that he wanted to play. He talked about a painful treatment that he had tried in an effort to return to the lineup. "My knee is so swollen I have to have four shots in it," Cepeda informed Milton Gross of the *New York Post*. "They take out the water [fluid] and it hurt like a son-of-a-gun. You think I do that if I don't want to play?"

No matter what he did, Cepeda couldn't keep himself in the lineup. By season's end, he had appeared in only thirty-three games. Worse yet, his final batting average read a paltry .176. Cepeda would have to read and hear about that awful number time and time again during the off-season— .176. He was determined not to repeat that number in 1966.

# Chapter Seven

# Two's a Crowd at First Base

Cepeda reported to spring training in 1966 sporting a much different physique. He had worked out hard over the winter, dropping 20 pounds of unneeded weight. By carrying around fewer pounds, he hoped to put less stress on his knees. Orlando looked better, and felt better.

As spring training progressed, Cepeda learned that the Giants had a new plan in mind for him. They wanted to make Willie McCovey, their top left-handed slugger, their everyday first baseman. That was great for McCovey, but meant that Cepeda would have to find another place to play. How about the outfield? The Giants told Orlando that he would have to compete for the team's left field job. It would not be given to him.

Manager Herman Franks insinuated that Cepeda was no longer one of his nine best players, and therefore not deserving of a starting role with the team. When Cepeda suggested the Giants trade him, Franks claimed that no other teams were interested in him. So it would be the outfield, or nothing, for Cepeda.

One reporter said that, as a result of McCovey taking his job at first base, Cepeda wouldn't talk to him anymore. Cepeda denied the charge. "Willie McCovey is my friend," Cepeda told Stan Isaacs of *Newsday*. Although Orlando did not always get along with Willie Mays, his relationship with McCovey continued to be good.

Still, the change to the outfield did not please Cepeda, who was trying to come back from knee problems. Playing the outfield would require more running and put more stress on his bad knee. Furthermore, Cepeda had been the Giants' regular first baseman for most of the past seven seasons. In 1962, the Giants had won the National League pennant with Cepeda playing first base—and McCovey in left field. Orlando thought to himself: why would the Giants tinker with a formula that had worked so well in the past?

In the first few spring training games, Orlando looked awful in the outfield. He made two errors in one game. He had trouble getting good jumps on fly balls, especially deep drives hit over his head. Some reporters even criticized him for not trying hard enough. In their eyes, he was "going through the motions."

Some of the officials in the Giants' organization questioned Cepeda's effort and desire. They felt he did not act like an adult. They even wondered about his intelligence. The criticism of Cepeda was wrapped up best in the following passage written by Stan Isaacs of *Newsday* during the spring of 1966:

*On the record, Cepeda should be ranked in the superstar class. He is regarded, instead, as a ballplayer with magnificent ability who hasn't taken advantage of his talents. He is considered to be a baby, a brooder, a dummy who does the wrong thing at the wrong time.*

*A baby. A dummy.* These were words that stung. Still, Cepeda tried to handle the criticism as best as he could. "I want people to like me but I don't care," Cepeda told sportswriter Joe Krupinski during spring training. "The critics aren't important."

Cepeda reached rock-bottom when he made two errors in one game. His pride was now at stake. Fortunately, the embarrassment seemed to motivate him. He started to play the field with more effort and desire. He worked harder at playing left field. He now seemed determined to make himself into a capable defensive outfielder.

Orlando also worked hard in the clubhouse. For an hour each day, he lifted 250-pound barbells with his legs. The exercises strengthened his legs and knees, which had become weakened by past injuries. Cepeda hoped that lifting weights would prevent him from getting injured in the future.

When the regular season began, Cepeda was not in left field. Herman Franks picked Len Gabrielson, a mediocre player who wasn't nearly as talented as Cepeda, to start the season in the outfield. Cepeda wasn't at first base, either. He was on the bench—apparently because he wasn't one of Herman Franks' best players anymore—and unhappy about it. He once again asked the Giants to trade him. Rumors soon started that had the Giants sending Cepeda on his way. One rumor had him going to the Los Angeles Dodgers for left-handed pitcher Claude Osteen. Another rumor had him going to the Chicago Cubs for pitcher Dick Ellsworth, also a veteran left-hander. If that trade were to happen, it would be a good one for Orlando. He enjoyed hitting at Chicago's Wrigley Field, which favored a hitter who could pound the ball into the outfield gaps with power. Cepeda was just that kind of hitter.

The Giants were apparently ready to make the trade, but the Cubs backed out. Chicago manager Leo Durocher supposedly asked the Giants to give the Cubs an extra player in the trade. The Giants said no, killing the deal.

In the meantime, the Giants gave Cepeda more playing time as a way of "showcasing" him to other teams. In early May, the Giants traveled to St. Louis to play the Cardinals in the final series of games to be played at the old Busch Stadium. In the last two games of the series, the Giants started Cepeda at first base. Cepeda banged out a grand slam home run in one game, followed by two hits and two RBIs in the next. The hitting spree helped the Giants cap off a three-game sweep of the Cardinals.

After the game, Cepeda walked down the runway that led from the dugout to the Giants' clubhouse. He was accompanied by Juan Marichal, his closest friend on the team. Marichal put his arm around Cepeda's shoulder and assured him that the Giants wouldn't trade him now. Not after the kind of series he had put together against the Cardinals.

A few moments later, Cepeda arrived in the clubhouse, where manager Herman Franks approached him. Cepeda thought Franks was about to offer him some words of thanks or encouragement after his performance against the Cardinals. Not quite. Instead, Franks had some news for him. Orlando no longer belonged to the Giants; he had been traded, but not to the Cubs, as had been rumored. No, he was going to the Cardinals, the same team that he and the Giants had just defeated.

Giants' vice-president Charles "Chub" Feeney and Cardinals' general manager Bob Howsam had actually agreed to the trade a day earlier, but wanted to wait until the end of the series to announce it officially. In exchange for Cepeda, the Cardinals gave the Giants Ray Sadecki, a left-handed pitcher who had won only six games and lost fifteen the previous year. That was it, a straight-up, one-for-one deal. Sadecki for Cepeda, a onetime Rookie of the Year and nearly the MVP in 1960. It would turn out to be one of the best trades the Cardinals ever made, and one of the worst for the Giants.

For the first time in his baseball life, Cepeda had experienced the feelings of rejection that come with being traded. He sat next to his locker in the Giants' clubhouse and felt tears running down his cheeks. "I cried for two days," Cepeda told Dwight Chapin of the *San Francisco Examiner.* "My wife cried, my mother cried—it was Mother's Day." It all made for an unhappy holiday.

The trade not only came as a shock to Cepeda but surprised many fans and followers of the team, given the comments of Giants' president and owner Horace Stoneham over the winter. "We have no plans to trade Cepeda," Stoneham had told *The Sporting News* in November. "He's not available as far as we're concerned." In reality, Stoneham did not want to trade Cepeda at all. But he had decided to listen to both his manager and general manager. Herman Franks and Chub Feeney both favored the idea of moving Cepeda to another team.

Orlando felt rejected by the Giants, but his new team did its best to make him feel welcome in St. Louis. The Cardinals offered to tear up Cepeda's old contract with San Francisco, which had cut his salary to $40,000. They agreed to give him a new deal, which would pay him $53,000—the same amount of money the Giants had paid him the previous year before cutting his salary. They also told him that he wouldn't have to worry about playing the outfield. Cepeda could concentrate on being the Cardinals' everyday first baseman. He would also be the team's number-four hitter—or cleanup hitter—the man expected to drive in runs the way Willie Mays had done for the Giants.

Playing in his first game with St. Louis, Orlando made a terrific first impression. He delivered a sacrifice fly, a single, and a home run in Bob Gibson's 8-0 win over the Cubs. The home run was especially meaningful to the Cardinals, who had been searching for a true cleanup hitter, one who could regularly hit the ball out of the park. Cepeda would fill that role very nicely.

Fans in St. Louis liked Orlando almost immediately. They appreciated the way that he smiled and laughed. They liked his willingness to talk to fans at games. To them, he seemed like a nice man with a good attitude. In other words, he was nothing like the person that some people in San Francisco had made him out to be.

Unfortunately, Cepeda's season—and career—almost came to an end a month after the trade took place. During pregame batting practice, Phillies outfielder Johnny Callison hit a ball that struck Orlando just above the right eye. If the ball had hit him a bit lower, Cepeda might have been blinded permanently. As it was, the injury left his eye swollen shut and kept him out of action for the next two weeks.

Cepeda bounced back well from the injury, showing little fear at the plate. He hit incredibly well for the Cardinals, lifting his average into the .330s by late July. Cepeda's batting average was even more remarkable considering that his bad right knee prevented him from collecting any infield or "leg" base hits. Orlando had to earn every hit by driving the ball past the infielders into the outfield.

Cepeda's early days in a St. Louis uniform gave him some special satisfaction, as well. On June 29, Orlando hit a 500-foot home run against his former Giant teammates. The long ball, the first to reach the upper deck of the Cardinals' new Busch Memorial Stadium, provided St. Louis with the winning run in a 2-1 victory over the Giants.

Cepeda's outstanding play in St. Louis led some writers to criticize the Giants for making a bad trade. One writer called the deal of Cepeda for Ray Sadecki the "worst trade of the century"—from San Francisco's perspective, that is. Giants' vice-president Chub Feeney tried to defend the team's decision to trade Cepeda. "We have Willie McCovey, and we feel Willie McCovey is a better fielder at first base," Feeney explained to Stan Isaacs of *Newsday.* "Cepeda didn't particularly love playing the outfield, and he certainly was inadequate out there." Feeney added that Cepeda's recent knee operation had hurt his trade value, causing other teams to be cautious about what they might give up for an injured player.

Feeney's explanations certainly made sense. But one question remained. Since Cepeda's trade value had fallen off so much because of his knee surgery, why didn't the Giants wait to make a trade? Wouldn't it have been smarter to play Cepeda every day at first base and show other teams that his knee was healthy, and then trade him? That way, the Giants might have gotten more than an inconsistent pitcher like Ray Sadecki in return.

During his days in San Francisco, some of the Giants had questioned Cepeda's desire to play. They wondered if he worked hard enough. In St. Louis, there was no such criticism. According to Cardinals' team trainer Clarence "Bob" Bauman, Orlando usually arrived at the ballpark about five hours prior to game time. He would go through a rigorous workout on his right knee, including a set of special exercises and a series of weightlifting routines. Bauman also fitted Cepeda with a special shoe that contained 23 pounds of lead. Sitting at the edge of a rubbing table, Orlando would have to raise his weighted foot until his leg was parallel with the ground. He repeated this painful exercise fifty times. After the game, Cepeda would return to the trainer's room and work on the knee some more. No one could question his work ethic now.

The 1966 season brought other changes to Orlando's life. In past years, he had generally been known by the nickname, "The Baby Bull." That name was starting to lose out in popularity to another nickname, one that was influenced by his love of music. A one-time drummer in his own band, Cepeda enjoyed listening to jazz and Latin American music. He owned a personal collection of nearly 6,000 albums and an elaborate stereo set-up. He also owned a portable phonograph, which he usually brought to the stadium. When he played his albums in the Cardinals' clubhouse, he sometimes went into a little Latino dance called a "cha cha." That was the nickname that former Giants' teammate Johnny Antonelli had given him during his days in San Francisco, but it never really caught on. Now that he was with the Cardinals, more and more people were calling him "Cha Cha."

In the meantime, Cepeda continued to hit National League pitching at an incredible rate. On July 31, his batting average stood at .339, the top figure in the league. As the season headed into August, Cepeda started thinking about winning the batting crown. It was something that hadn't been done by a Cardinal player since 1957, when Hall of Famer Stan Musial earned his *seventh* batting title. Cepeda outlined a simple formula for winning his first major league hitting crown. "I've been consistent," Orlando said in an interview with Neal Russo of *The Sporting News*, "and that's what you have to do, get at least one hit a day, if you're going for the batting title. Look at Roberto Clemente and Tony Oliva. They get their hit a game." Clemente had already won three National League batting crowns; Oliva, a native of Cuba, had won two American League titles.

In the minor leagues, Cepeda had won two league batting titles of his own. Yet, as well as Cepeda had played for the Giants, he had usually not hit for a particularly high average. So why the change in St. Louis? Orlando cited two reasons for his improved play. One was the weather. He had never liked playing in San Francisco, where it was often cold and windy, especially during night games at Candlestick Park. He preferred to play in the heat and humidity of St. Louis, which was similar to the playing conditions of his native Puerto Rico. The other reason? He liked his new teammates in the St. Louis clubhouse. "I never used to play cards with the guys in San Francisco," Orlando told *The Sporting News*, recalling a Giants' clubhouse that was often divided by race. "Baseball is a tough game to play, but you have to have fun when you play it." In St. Louis, the players hung out together, regardless of whether they were white, black, or Latin American.

As much as Cepeda liked his new teammates, they appreciated his presence even more. His heavy hitting helped the Cardinals improve from being a sub-.500 team in 1965 to a team that was now contending in the National League. "What made our club click," catcher Tim McCarver told Neal Russo of *The Sporting News* in August, "can be summed up in one word: Cepeda. He gave us a fighting chance. Every club seems to have a big clutch hitter. The Giants have Willie Mays. The Phillies have Richie Allen. The Braves have Hank Aaron. Cepeda's *our* big man."

Cepeda was their big man, but he couldn't carry the team all season long. Since the Cardinals didn't have much power besides Cepeda, and no other .300 hitters in their lineup, opposing pitchers realized they could pitch around "The Baby Bull." In August and September, Cepeda's batting average fell off considerably. As a result, there would be no batting crown for Cepeda, and no pennant for the Cardinals.

Yet, Cepeda's performance over the last five months of the season created optimism for the future. The Cardinals started to dream. What would "Cha Cha" be able do over a full season, one that was uninterrupted by trade or injury? The National League would soon find out.

# Chapter Eight

# Starring in St. Louis

Even though the sportswriters had named him "Comeback Player of the Year," Orlando reported to spring training determined to improve on his 1966 statistics. After a great start, he had slumped during the second half of the season. The poor finish motivated him to return to Puerto Rico to continue playing baseball. "That's why I played winter ball," Orlando told Jack Herman of *The Sporting News* during spring training. "I wanted to get back in the groove. Now everything is set."

The Cardinals had also helped Cepeda by acquiring another slugger during the off-season. The addition of right fielder Roger Maris, who had set the major league record for most home runs in a single season only six years earlier, figured to take some of the pressure away from Cepeda. The Cardinals would no longer be asking Orlando to supply all of the power in the Redbird lineup.

The addition of Maris had a positive impact on Cepeda early in the season. On May 5, Orlando ripped a two-run homer against Chicago's Ken Holtzman. The next game, he socked two home runs against Curt Simmons. Cepeda wrapped up the finale of the three-game series with another home run against rookie pitcher Rich Nye. With six hits in 11 at-bats against the Cubs, Cepeda lifted his batting average to .384.

In his first twenty-seven games, Cepeda drove in 25 runs—an astonishing rate of success. With Cepeda leading the way, the Cardinals were scoring nearly five runs per game. In 1966, they had averaged only three and a half runs per contest.

On Father's Day, Orlando enjoyed one of the most satisfying days of his major league career. With the Cardinals and Giants locked up in a 1-1 tie at Candlestick Park in San Francisco, Cepeda came to the plate with one man on in the top of the eighth inning. He would have to face tough right-hander Gaylord Perry, one of the players who felt that Cepeda did not always try hard enough during his days in the Bay Area. Perry threw Cepeda one of his trademark spitballs, an illegal pitch that was tougher to hit than a standard fastball. The pitch didn't bother Cepeda. He smashed it over the screened outfield fence at Candlestick Park. The two-run homer helped the Cardinals to a 4-1 win over the Giants.

Cepeda's game-winning home run felt even more special since it had come against his former team. He had not forgotten the criticism that had come from some of his former teammates and other members of the Giants' organization. "The home run made me happy," Cepeda explained to Neal Russo of *The Sporting News*, "because they accused me so much, when I played for the Giants, of not hitting in the clutch."

No one could dispute that his latest home run had come in the clutch. More importantly, it allowed the red-hot Cardinals to move into first place in the National League. With nine wins in their last eleven games, no team was playing better than the Redbirds.

Cepeda wasn't just playing well offensively. He has also improved his fielding at first base, where he skillfully scooped up low throws from the other infielders. In addition, Cepeda was becoming a strong influence in the Cardinal clubhouse and dugout. Orlando liked to cheer on his teammates, even when they were struggling. He encouraged the other Cardinals, helping to put them in the right frame of mind. "He's always optimistic," outfielder Lou Brock told Leonard Shecter of *Sport Magazine*. "You can get bugged [upset] in this game, you know. But Cepeda is always there, very energetic, full of fire, and it's catching."

Orlando's enthusiasm seemed to catch on with one player, in particular. As the team's first baseman, Cepeda played just a few feet to the right of Julián "The Phantom" Javier. The Cardinals' second baseman hadn't hit higher than .241 over the last three years. A sensitive and shy man, Javier seemed to lack confidence. Cepeda sensed that, and decided to do something about it. He spoke Spanish with the quiet Dominican, who had trouble with the English language. He became friendly with Javier, calling him by his other nickname, "Hoolie." He told him how important he was to the Cardinals. "We need you, Hoolie," Cepeda said to Javier again and again.

Other players on the team noticed the relationship between Cepeda and Javier. "They're good for each other," observed shortstop Dal Maxvill, whose locker was located between Orlando and Julián. "Orlando is such a great cheerleader that he gets others to put out more. He has a knack for making suggestions in a nice way," Maxvill told Neal Russo of *The Sporting News*.

Cepeda's encouragement worked on Javier. The veteran second baseman finished the 1967 season with a .281 batting average. That represented a 53-point improvement over the previous year. It was also the highest average of Javier's eight-year career in the major leagues.

Cepeda tried to make baseball more enjoyable for all of his teammates and coaches. One day, third base coach Joe Schultz started calling the Cardinals "El Birdos." It was a strange nickname that combined Spanish and English. (Schultz had managed Winter League teams in Latin America, where he learned a few Spanish words.) Cepeda decided to have some fun with the name. Rather than try to correct Schultz's Spanish, he decided to make the nickname a rallying cry for the team. After games that the Cardinals won, Cepeda would run into the clubhouse, jump on top of a table or clothing trunk, and start shouting, "Who wins the game?" The other players would respond in unison, "El Birdos." Cepeda would then lead the team in a variety of cheers, often making them up as he went along. Some of the cheers were funny; some poked fun at his former team in San Francisco.

Even if Cepeda himself had a bad game, he never allowed his struggles to interfere with his role as the team's unofficial cheerleader. "What really has impressed me about 'Cha Cha' is that even if he's gone 0-for-4 and we win, he gets on the trunk and leads the cheers," Dal Maxvill told *The Sporting News.* "If he goes 4-for-4 and we lose, he just quietly undresses. It's easy for superstars to sit back and feel that they've done their job . . . Instead, Orlando always is trying to inspire the rest of us." The cheers helped make the St. Louis clubhouse loose and relaxed. In turn, the Cardinals performed better as a team.

Orlando's growing value to the Cardinals was perhaps best illustrated by a scene that took place on the team bus during the 1967 season. After checking out of the Park Sheraton Hotel in New York, the Cardinal players gathered on the bus that was scheduled to take them to Shea Stadium to play the Mets. All of the players arrived at the bus on time—except for one. Cepeda was nowhere to be found. A bellhop, carrying some of Cepeda's equipment, soon came by and told the players that their first baseman was on his way. The team waited, and waited some more, before several players started to grow impatient. A few of the players shouted toward the bus driver, "Let's go, let's go." The bus driver was about to follow their orders when another player stood up. It was Bob Gibson, the team's best pitcher and a future Hall of Famer. "We're waiting for Cepeda," Gibson announced boldly to his teammates. "The pitchers aren't leaving without him." So the bus waited until Cepeda arrived. That's how much Orlando had come to mean to the Cardinals.

Cepeda continued to lead the Redbirds on the field. At the All-Star break, Cepeda owned a league-leading .356 average. Not so coincidentally, the Cardinals enjoyed a three-and-a-half-game lead in the pennant race. As the season headed into the second week of August, Orlando's average had dipped somewhat, but he was still sporting a .334 mark. Better yet, he led all major league hitters with 85 RBIs. He had given the Cardinals something that they had lacked since their championship season of 1964: a dangerous cleanup hitter.

With Cepeda driving in loads of key runs, other National League contenders had trouble keeping pace with the Cardinals. The Reds had endured a major blow in June, when their star shortstop from Cuba, Leo Cárdenas, broke his finger. The Pirates, hopeful of contending after the off-season pickup of Puerto Rican ace Juan Pizarro, were disappointed by the left-hander's performance in the starting rotation. In early August, the Giants lost their best pitcher, Juan Marichal, to injury. The "Dominican Dandy" would pitch only a handful of innings the rest of the way.

In the meantime, the Cardinals stayed healthy and started to run away with the National League pennant race. By August 15, the Cards opened up a double-digit lead of ten and a half games over both the Reds and Atlanta Braves. Less than two weeks later, Cepeda drove in his 100th run of the season. That was considered an excellent total for a full season, but the schedule hadn't even reached September!

The Cardinals continued to own a huge lead over their National League rivals. Even a mid-season injury to pitching ace Bob Gibson couldn't slow them down. As they headed into their game on September 18 against the Phillies, the

Cardinals held a twelve-and-a-half-game lead over the second-place Giants and had reduced their "magic number" to one. In other words, the Cardinals needed to win only one more game, or have the Giants lose one more game to officially clinch the National League pennant.

With Gibson recovered from a broken leg and making his third start since returning from the disabled list, the Cardinals felt good about their chances of clinching that day. True to form, Gibson held the Phillies scoreless over the first five innings. In the top of the sixth, the Cardinals put together a rally. Lou Brock doubled in St. Louis' first run. Julián Javier added an RBI single of his own. With one out, the Phillies then walked Cepeda intentionally, bringing Mike "Moon Man" Shannon to the plate. The Cardinal third baseman pounded out a double, scoring another run. When Philadelphia's Octavio "Cookie" Rojas threw wildly, Cepeda scored the fourth run of the inning.

A 4-0 lead seemed safe with Gibson on the mound. It was. Gibson held the Phillies to only three hits in pitching a complete game. The Cardinals won 5-1, putting them in the World Series for the first time since 1964.

The Cardinal players raced to the clubhouse, where they soon found Cepeda leading the cheers. He called the Cardinals "the greatest team ever to play in the National League." Orlando also shouted out adjectives to describe his Cardinal teammates. He used words like "beautiful" and "wonderful."

Those were good words to describe Roger Maris, one of Orlando's new teammates in 1967. The Cardinals had acquired Maris in the hope that he would help Cepeda produce better offensive numbers. The plan had worked. With Maris around to remove some of the pressure, Cepeda had put together one of the best seasons of his major league career.

Yet, none of this would have happened if not for another trade, the one that had made Cepeda an ex-Giant and a current Cardinal. The Giants had once criticized Cepeda for his inability to deliver clutch hitting when they needed it the most. This was the same Cepeda who had come up with important, run-scoring hits in five games against the Giants in 1967. The Cardinals had won all five of those games, helping them win the pennant over the Giants.

Although the trade from San Francisco to St. Louis had hurt his pride in the short term, it turned out to be the best thing for Cepeda. "Over there I am nothing," Orlando told Arthur Daley of the *New York Times,* recalling his days with the Giants. "Here I am something." The Cardinals certainly agreed.

With the pennant clinched, only one piece of suspense remained for the Cardinals. Who would they face in the World Series? Given the incredible four-team pennant race in the American League, the Cardinals would have to wait out the final week and a half of the regular season. Heading into the games of September 19, the Boston Red Sox, Detroit Tigers, and Minnesota Twins were tied for first place, with the Chicago White Sox only a half-game back.

It wasn't until the final day of the season that the Cardinals found out the identity of their World Series opponents. The Red Sox outlasted the White Sox, Tigers, and Twins, finally ending what sportswriters had called "The Great Race." Much like the Cardinals, the Red Sox had been considered an incredible long shot to win the pennant.

Strangely, the Red Sox's players didn't seem to have much respect for the Cardinals, who had actually won nine more games than Boston during the season. Some of the players would criticize the Cardinals throughout the Series, predicting an easy victory for Boston. Boston's boastful words only made the St. Louis players more determined to win it all.

The World Series opened up at Boston's historic Fenway Park. Orlando had never played a game at the old stadium, which favored right-handed pull hitters with its short distance to left field. The large wall in left, known as the "Green Monster," gave power hitters an inviting target.

Unlike many power hitters, Cepeda was not a pull hitter. He liked to drive the ball into the gaps, in left-center and right-center field. He had to keep reminding himself not to try to pull the ball at Fenway. He needed to maintain his usual style of hitting to be successful.

Unfortunately, Orlando gave into the temptation of pulling the ball toward the "Green Monster." He went hitless in Game One. It didn't matter, though, as the Cardinals won the game behind the standout pitching of ace Bob Gibson. In Game Two, Cepeda went hitless again. This time it mattered a little bit more. The Red Sox scored three runs in the seventh to cement an easy 5-0 win.

Cepeda wasn't the only Cardinal hitter to fail. As a team, St. Louis managed just one hit against Boston's twenty-two-game winner, Jim Lonborg. The Red Sox's ace had pitched no-hit ball until Julián Javier doubled with two outs in the eighth inning. So, it wasn't like Cepeda was the main reason the Cardinals had lost. But when the team didn't hit, writers and fans looked to The Baby Bull first. He was the Cardinals' number-one home run hitter and RBI-man. He was the player they expected to carry the team.

He hadn't done that in the first two games. He had come up empty in seven at-bats at Fenway Park. To make matters worse, he had managed to hit only one ball out of the infield. Although he had tried not to give in to the habit of trying to pull pitches at Fenway, many of the Red Sox players felt he had done just that.

Orlando tried to remain positive. "I have so much confidence," the struggling first baseman told reporters. "I always think I'll hit tomorrow and tomorrow and tomorrow." The day after tomorrow, the Cardinals would have the advantage of playing in their home stadium—St. Louis' Busch Memorial Stadium.

In Game Three, Cepeda went hitless in his first three at-bats before finally breaking out of his slump. Now that he was back in his home ballpark in St. Louis, he had no reason to try to pull the ball. Facing reliever Dan Osinski, "Cha Cha" doubled off the wall in deep right-center field, scoring Roger Maris. The opposite-field hit capped off a 5-2 win for the Cardinals.

The eighth-inning hit seemed to relax Cepeda. He pounded out another double in Game Four, helping the Cardinals stage a two-run rally on their way to a 6-0 victory. The win put St. Louis one game away from the world championship.

But the Red Sox would not give up easily. They rallied to win the next two games, as Cepeda picked up only a measly infield single in nine at-bats. The two Boston wins set the stage for a decisive seventh game at Fenway Park—winner-take-all.

The Red Sox had the advantage of playing the game at home, but that didn't stop the Cardinals from jumping on Boston ace Jim Lonborg, who had to pitch on only two days' rest instead of the usual three days. The Redbirds scored two runs in the third, two runs in the fifth, and three in the sixth before a tired Lonborg left the game. In the meantime, Cardinals' ace Bob Gibson pitched one of his typically dominant, strikeout-filled games. Gibson fanned ten Red Sox on his way to a complete game win, making the Cardinals the champions of baseball.

For the first time in his career, Cepeda could call himself a world champion. On the down side, he had finished the Series with only three hits in 29 at-bats and a terrible batting average of .103. He drove in only one run. His hitting in this Series was even worse than it had been in the 1962 Fall Classic.

Why did he struggle so badly after such a great regular season? Well, Red Sox's pitching deserved some of the credit. Knowing that he liked to hit curveballs, Boston pitchers threw him mostly fastballs and sliders. And when they did throw him a curve, they kept it outside of the strike zone. Orlando ended up chasing some of those bad curves and became an easy out for the Red Sox.

Fortunately for the Cardinals, Cepeda's difficulties hadn't interfered with the team's effort to win the Series. They also wouldn't interfere with the results of the Most Valuable Player award (MVP) voting, which was based solely on regular season performance and not the World Series. On November 7, Cepeda found out that he had been named the winner of the prestigious award. That wasn't surprising. But the voting was expected to be fairly close. It wasn't. Every one of the twenty writers who covered the National League on a regular basis felt that Cepeda was more valuable to his team than any other player. Orlando easily beat out teammate Tim McCarver, who finished second in the balloting, and Puerto Rico's most well-known player, Roberto Clemente, who finished third. Clemente had outhit Cepeda by 32 points, but the writers still felt that Cepeda had done more to help his team win.

In sweeping the vote, Cepeda became the first second major league player to win both the Rookie of the Year and the MVP in unanimous fashion. He also became only the second National League player to earn all of the MVP votes. In the thirty-six-year history of the award, only Carl Hubbell of the New York Giants had accomplished the feat previously, with his award coming in 1936. Even the legendary likes of Hank Aaron, Stan Musial, and Willie Mays had never been unanimous winners of the MVP.

Orlando also joined exclusive company in the American League, where only four players had ever swept the MVP vote. Three of the four were present or future Hall of Famers:

Hank Greenberg, Mickey Mantle, and Frank Robinson. Cepeda had taken his place next to some of the game's greatest legends.

More importantly, Cepeda had kept the MVP award in his native Puerto Rico. In 1966, Roberto Clemente had captured the same award. "It's a great honor for me and my people," Cepeda proudly told sportswriter George Vecsey.

Shortly after the announcement of the MVP selection, Orlando decided to lend his time toward helping the Latino community in the United States. He agreed to participate in a tour of American schools. He wanted to remind the students that they could be successful, too.

On a snowy day in early December, Cepeda paid a visit to Public School 83 in East Harlem, New York. It was a fitting place for a native Puerto Rican like Cepeda. After all, the school was named after Luis Muñoz Marín, a great social activist whom some called the "George Washington of Puerto Rico." In addition, 75 percent of the students at P.S. 83 were Puerto Rican. They would now have a chance to meet one of the most famous Puerto Ricans alive.

Unfortunately, most of the fourth, fifth, and sixth-grade students who watched Cepeda speak in the school auditorium did not know much about him. Some of the students had never heard of him. Cepeda played in St. Louis; the Bronx-based students followed local legends like Mickey Mantle, who was the most well-known player for either the hometown Mets or Yankees. Still, the chance to see Cepeda meant something to the youngsters because they shared a common bond with him. "We all like him," sixth-grader Harry Oliveras told the *New York Times,* "because he's from our same background."

Orlando started his speech by speaking in Spanish. He told the assembly of 350 students that he had never walked through snow before. He then repeated his words in English. He told the students about how difficult life can be and reminded them about the importance of working hard. If Cepeda himself had not worked hard, he would never have become a successful major league ballplayer.

After completing his talk at the school, Cepeda walked to a local boys' club where he was scheduled to conduct a baseball clinic. As he waited for the group of boys to arrive, he picked up a basketball in the gymnasium and started shooting baskets. It reminded him of his days as a teenager, when he played basketball instead of baseball. A short time later, the boys arrived. They immediately stationed themselves under the hoop and rim, hoping they could pick up a rebound and pass the ball back to the celebrity who was visiting them. Cepeda and the boys smiled and laughed.

A few minutes later, the baseball clinic began. Orlando began teaching the youngsters the fundamentals of playing first base. One great athlete. Two sports. Two visits. One memorable day in the Bronx.

# Chapter Nine

# Trying to Repeat

As well as Cepeda had played in 1967, it would be tough for him to match that performance in 1968. After a shaky start to the new season, Orlando hit a major slump during the month of July. His bat looked so slow that manager Red Schoendienst took him out of the lineup for two straight games on July 20 and 21. Prior to that, he had played every inning of every game. Cepeda's teammates tried to ease the tension by joking with him, calling him "El Bencho." There was no such word in Spanish, but Cepeda understood the message. He smiled, knowing that his mates were teasing him in a friendly way. But underneath the smile, the benching hurt Cepeda's pride.

If Orlando had any doubts about the difficulties of trying to repeat what he had done the previous summer, they ended on July 22. Something strange happened that day, something that never would have happened during his dream season of 1967.

The Cardinals trailed the Phillies by two runs as they came to bat in the ninth inning. Cepeda, by now returned to the starting lineup, was scheduled to bat with the potential tying runs on first and second base. Manager Red Schoendienst told Orlando to hold on. He called his slugging first baseman back and told him that he was taking him out of the game for a pinch-hitter. Schoendienst sent up Lou Brock, who singled in a run. The Cardinals ended up scoring three runs to win the game, 5-4. They completed the comeback without Cepeda.

Orlando was stunned by Schoendienst's decision. He had never been removed for a pinch-hitter in 5,548 official major league at-bats. "This is a new experience for me," Cepeda told *The Sporting News.* "I wanted to bat. I was mad at first."

If Cepeda had been replaced with a pinch-hitter during his early major league days in San Francisco, he might have stayed mad and said something he shouldn't have. Now a member of the Cardinals, Orlando was older and more mature. He actually went on to defend Schoendienst's decision. "You never stop learning in this game. The manager made the right move," Cepeda said calmly. "I haven't been hitting. [Brock's] been hitting well."

Cepeda's classy reaction to Schoendienst's decision did not go unnoticed. In its August 10th editorial, *The Sporting News* pointed out that Cepeda had been "quite ordinary" as a player that year. "Yet, in our opinion," *The Sporting News* went on to say, "Cepeda proved himself a better man or, at least, a better person this year because of a remarkable incident that occurred the other day." After describing the pinch-hitting incident and Orlando's reaction to it, *The Sporting News* gave Cepeda its highest praise. "We hope that the great and the near-great in baseball remember Orlando's words. It takes a great man to swallow bitter disappointment and acknowledge that the manager's judgment must prevail."

Although Cepeda was showing great maturity in handling his baseball career, he was having problems in other areas. In June, the Internal Revenue Service had revealed that Cepeda owed over $9,000 in back taxes. The taxes dated back to 1965. As the season continued, tax collectors placed more and more pressure on him to pay up his debt.

Perhaps bothered by his tax problems, Cepeda posted sagging statistics during the season. But the play of the Cardinals didn't. On September 15, the Cardinals faced the Houston Astros, with a chance to guarantee no worse than a tie for the National League pennant. Young left-hander and future Hall of Famer Steve Carlton pitched well in making the start. Star center fielder Curt Flood led the offensive charge with five hits in five at-bats. The Cardinals defeated the Astros, 7-4, to clinch a tie for the National League pennant.

Now all the Cardinals had to do was await the outcome of the Giants' game in San Francisco against the Reds. If the Reds could defeat the Giants, the Cardinals would be guaranteed the National League pennant all to themselves. Several of the Cardinal players gathered in the room of trainer Bob Bauman. There they would listen to a special telephone hook-up that would deliver the radio play-by-play of the game between the Giants and Reds.

By the time the hook-up had been made, the Giants' game had moved to the seventh inning. There was no score. Within a few minutes, the Reds put a run up on the board. They soon added three more. The Reds held on for a 4-0 victory. The win meant little for the Reds, but meant everything for the Cardinals. They were now officially National League champions for the second straight summer.

The Cardinals moved their celebration to the clubhouse. Cepeda jumped up onto one of the tables in the room and started leading cheers. His teammates joined in. Some of the players threw buckets of water and champagne. Other players became so excited that they ripped T-shirts from the backs of their teammates. Still others dragged their teammates into the showers, turning the water on full blast. They were all different ways for the Cardinals to celebrate their return trip to the World Series, where they would take on the American League champion Detroit Tigers.

Much like they did in 1967, the Cardinals won the first game of the World Series without much contribution from Cepeda. "Cha Cha" went 0-for-4 in the opener. But that wasn't the big story of the game. The story was the pitching of Bob Gibson, who set a World Series record by striking out seventeen Tigers. Gibson also outdueled Detroit's top pitcher, Denny McLain, who had won thirty-one games during the regular season.

Cepeda managed to crank up his bat in Game Two. He collected two hits in four at-bats, but his offensive surge turned out to be in vain. The Tigers crushed the Cardinals, 8-1.

Throughout his major league career, Orlando had been known as an outstanding hitter. He was particularly well-known for hitting home runs. But in fourteen World Series games, he had not hit a single home run. It was unusual for him to go that many games during the regular season without hitting one out. The Cardinals wondered whether he would ever deliver the longball in one of these important World Series games.

With the Cardinals leading the Tigers 4-3 in the seventh inning of Game Three, Cepeda stepped to the plate. St. Louis had placed runners on second and third with no one out. The pressure was on Cepeda. He needed to lift the ball into the air, just deep enough to score the speedy Curt Flood from third. That would give the Cardinals a much-needed insurance run.

Cepeda did more than lift the ball into the air. He lifted it into the left-field stands. His first home run in World Series play gave the Cardinals a four-run lead on their way to a 7-3 victory.

The Cardinals won the next game, too. Cepeda chipped in with a single, a walk, and a nifty one-handed catch near the first base dugout. A 10-1 romp gave St. Louis a lead of three-games-to-one in the Series.

Moving in for the kill in Game Five, the Cardinals put together an immediate rally in the first inning. Lou Brock doubled and scored on a single by Curt Flood. After Flood stole second, Cepeda rocked a delivery from Mickey Lolich into the left-center field stands. Cepeda's second World Series home run gave the Cardinals a 3-0 lead. It seemed that the Redbirds would win their second straight world championship in just a matter of a few innings.

Yet, in baseball, a three-run lead is not insurmountable. Unlike many other sports, the team that has the lead cannot "kill" the clock by stalling or using other delay tactics. The trailing team's batters must be retired twenty-seven times over the course of nine innings, regardless of how long it takes.

In the fourth inning, the Tigers scored two runs to make it a close game. In the seventh inning, Detroit rallied for three more runs. Even a great diving play by Cepeda on a smash by Jim Northrup couldn't prevent the game-changing rally. The Tigers went on to a stunning 5-3 victory.

The loss seemed to affect the Cardinals badly. They played poorly in the next game, losing 13-1 at Busch Memorial Stadium. Cepeda, with two hits in four at-bats, was one of the lone bright spots for St. Louis. All of a sudden, the Series was tied at three games apiece. Just as they had done in 1967, the Cardinals would have to play a seventh game.

Mickey Lolich and Bob Gibson pitched shutout ball over the first six innings. In the seventh, Gibson seemed well on his way to prolonging the shutout when he retired the first two batters. But Norm Cash and Willie Horton kept the inning alive with singles. Jim Northrup then hit a deep drive toward left-center field. It was a ball that Curt Flood, an excellent center fielder, would have caught most of the time. For some reason, Flood started in on the ball before retreating. By then it was too late. The ball landed untouched near the warning track. Both Cash and Horton scored, giving the Tigers the lead.

The Tigers tacked on another run when Bill Freehan doubled into the left-center field gap. Now trailing by three runs, the Cardinals had only three innings left to stage a comeback. They needed to put a couple of runners on base and hope that a slugger like Cepeda or Roger Maris could hit one out.

With a runner on second base and two men out in the seventh inning, Maris popped out. In his final two at-bats, Cepeda struck out and fouled out. Mike Shannon did hit a home run in bottom of the ninth inning, but it came with no one on base. It wasn't enough. Detroit held on for a 4-1 win. Unbelievably, the Tigers—and not the Cardinals—had won the world championship.

The loss devastated the Cardinals. Just a few days earlier, they seemed to be in full control of the Series. Holding a 3-0 lead in Game Five, they had been only eight innings away from winning the title. Cepeda was also in the midst of his best World Series ever, with two home runs, a team-leading six RBIs, and some flawless fielding at first base. But the fortunes of both Cepeda and the Cardinals had changed quickly over the final three games. For Cepeda, those final three games turned out to be an unpleasant ending to his days in a Cardinal uniform.

# Chapter Ten

# A Trade of Superstars

Orlando didn't know it, but Cardinal management had decided that he no longer fit into their plans for the future. Team officials noticed how he had slumped during the 1968 regular season. They were also becoming very concerned over one of his personal problems; his tax debt. They believed that his problems with the Internal Revenue Service would continue to affect his performance on the field.

Cardinals' general manager Bing Devine quietly began talking trades with other teams. At first, he didn't like the offers that other teams were making. As the Cardinals headed for another spring training camp in St. Petersburg, Cepeda remained St. Louis's property.

Cepeda didn't please Devine when he showed up late for spring training. The Cardinals fined their first baseman $250. Devine remained determined to find another team that would give him what he wanted for Cepeda.

All the while, most of the St. Louis media didn't realize that Cepeda was on the trading block. The team's beat writers figured that he would remain a Cardinal for the 1969 season. So the news of March 17, when Devine announced a trade of Cepeda, caught most Cardinal fans and followers by surprise.

In 1966, the Cardinals had acquired Cepeda in a straight-up, one-for-one trade. Now they were sending him away in another simple one-for-one deal. His destination? The Atlanta Braves. In return, the Cardinals received Joe

Torre, a hard-hitting catcher who could also play the infield. This was the same Joe Torre who would one day win a National League batting title for the Cards and eventually become a world championship manager with the New York Yankees.

The trade of Cepeda was not a popular one with most fans of the Cardinals. Some of them wrote angry letters to the *St. Louis Post-Dispatch* and *The Sporting News* complaining about the departure of one of the team's most popular players. The trade was also difficult for Cepeda to take. He asked Guillermo "Willie" Montanez, a rookie first baseman from Puerto Rico, to go to the Cardinals' clubhouse in St. Petersburg and pick up his things. Orlando didn't think he could handle a farewell scene in the clubhouse. "I didn't want to say goodbye to all the guys," Cepeda explained to Milton Gross of the *New York Post.* "What could I say to 'Hoot' [the nickname for Bob Gibson], Curt [Flood], Lou [Brock], Timmy [McCarver]? They're all my friends. We have such a good team. We have such fun together. It is not easy."

Cepeda couldn't understand why the Cardinals had decided to get rid of him after he had helped the team to two straight World Series appearances. "I don't know why they traded me," Cepeda admitted to the *New York Post.* "I'm only thirty-one. Maybe they figure I'm over the hill. When they trade you, they don't want you."

It was no easier for Orlando's wife, Ana, to take the news. "It takes so long to get used to a city, to make friends," Ana told Milton Gross. The trade also affected another member of the Cepeda family. Ana and Orlando's three-year-old son was confused. Orlando Xavier didn't completely understand what it meant to be "traded." The boy knew something had happened, but wasn't exactly sure what it was.

Although Cepeda was unhappy about leaving St. Louis, he soon realized that the trade wasn't all that bad. The

Braves played in a ballpark that was much more favorable to power hitters than St. Louis's Busch Memorial Stadium. Furthermore, the Braves had a good offensive ballclub, with terrific hitters like Hank Aaron and Rico Carty in the every-day lineup. That figured to make it easier on Cepeda, who wouldn't be asked to carry the team's offense. The trade also reunited Orlando with two familiar faces from his past. One of them was Felipe Alou, his good friend on the Giants who now played center field for the Braves. The other was Atlanta's manager, Luman "Lum" Harris, whom Cepeda had once played for in the Puerto Rican Winter League. Cepeda liked Harris, a fair man who treated blacks and Latinos the same as he did white players.

Some people in baseball thought the Cardinals had received the better end of the deal. They felt that Torre was more valuable because he could play many positions—catcher, first base, or third base; while Cepeda could play only first base. Torre was also young and on the rise while Cepeda was in his early thirties.

Cepeda disagreed with those arguments. "Torre's only two years younger than me," Orlando pointed out to sports-writer Maury Allen, "and I'm stronger." In fact, that's why the Braves wanted Cepeda. They needed another power hit-ter who could hit home runs frequently. Torre was more of a line drive hitter who hit singles and doubles with an occa-sional homerun.

The Braves had definite plans for Cepeda. They wanted Cepeda to bat behind their best hitter, cleanup man Hank Aaron. The Braves hoped that Cepeda would "protect" Aaron; in other words, opposing pitchers would be forced to throw Aaron better pitches to hit, so as not to walk him and have to face Cepeda with a runner on base. With Cepeda providing plenty of "protection," Aaron would enjoy a better season than he had in 1968. He would hit 44 home runs, compared to only 29 home runs in 1968.

Although Cepeda's new role with the Braves was an important one, it also meant that he would be paired with a more well-known superstar teammate for the second time in his career. As a result, Cepeda would receive less attention and publicity. "It's the same thing all over again here," Cepeda told sportswriter Maury Allen. "I used to hit behind Willie Mays [with the Giants]. Wherever I play, it seems I have to prove myself."

Cepeda started slowly at the plate for the Braves, but he did deliver some timely hits. Even though his batting average was hovering around the .200 mark, he drove in the game-winning run three times over the first two weeks of the season. He also tied up another game by hitting an important home run in the eighth inning. The Braves went on to win that game in the ninth inning.

After his relatively slow start at the plate, Orlando started to pick up hits more frequently. That was no surprise. The Braves knew that Cepeda could hit—and would hit even more as the season unfolded. But they might have been a bit stunned by the way he fielded his position at first base. That part of his game really stood out. His defensive play, which had always been overlooked, was finally earning him respect. Atlanta vice-president Paul Richards certainly took notice. Impressed by Cepeda's slick fielding, Richards felt motivated to call the Braves' infield of Cepeda, Felix "The Cat" Millán, Sonny Jackson, and Clete Boyer, the best in all of baseball.

On May 27, Cepeda made his most memorable defensive play. That day, the Braves played the Cardinals, Orlando's former team. Tim McCarver, a left-handed batter, faced Braves' pitcher Pat Jarvis. Since McCarver normally didn't pull the ball that severely, Cepeda was leaning his body toward second base. McCarver then rocked a pitch down the right field line, one of the hardest-hit balls Cepeda had ever seen. Even though Cepeda was expecting McCarver to hit the ball to his right, he quickly dove to his left and knocked down the line drive smash. Cepeda scrambled to his feet, picked up the ball, and beat McCarver to the bag. "It was the best play I've ever made," Cepeda told Wayne Minshew of *The Sporting News*. Pat Jarvis had one word to describe the play. "Unbelievable!"

Cepeda wasn't done that day. In the fifth inning, he delivered the game-winning hit with a run-scoring double. The Braves went on to beat the Cardinals, 5-3. Cepeda had once again sent a message to one of his former teams. *You made a mistake when you traded me.*

At the time of the trade, Orlando had felt shock and betrayal. Now he seemed happy in Atlanta. "I'm thirty-one years old, I'm rich, and I'm handsome, and I'm starting to hit," Cepeda said, joking with Phil Pepe of the *New York Post*. "What more could I want?"

Orlando was happy, and his enthusiastic attitude rubbed off on his new teammates. The other Braves players took note of his spirited style of play, appreciating the way he cheerfully encouraged his teammates. They benefited from his upbeat personality, just the way the Cardinals had for the last three seasons.

In the past, Cepeda had wanted better relationships with his manager. In Atlanta, he was getting along well with his new skipper. Unlike some of the managers that Orlando had struggled with in San Francisco, Luman Harris seemed to understand Cepeda. When a reporter asked Cepeda how a manager should handle him, Orlando gave a quick answer. "Leave him alone," Orlando said. Harris was doing just that.

Spurred on by the play of Cepeda, the Braves established themselves as one of the best teams in the National League's newly-formed Western Division. They contended for first place in the West, fighting off teams like the Giants, Reds, and Dodgers. As the season headed into September,

Cepeda's former team in San Francisco posed the biggest challenge to Atlanta.

On September 26, the Braves trailed the lowly San Diego Padres, one of the new expansion teams in the National League, by three runs. In the bottom of the third, the Braves loaded the bases. Rico Carty drew a walk, forcing in a run and bringing Cepeda to the plate. A few moments later, Cepeda crossed home plate himself. He had hit a bases-loaded home run—or a grand slam—giving the Braves a 5-3 lead. Atlanta went on to win the game, 10-4, and maintain a game-and-a-half lead over the Giants in the Western Division.

Cepeda's 22nd home run had helped the Braves win their seventh straight game. Just twenty games earlier, the Braves had trailed the division by two games. During that stretch, Cepeda was batting .286 with 13 RBIs. He was one of the biggest reasons why the Braves had won fourteen of their last seventeen games.

The Braves continued their series against the Padres on Saturday afternoon. Cepeda's bat fell quiet that day, but two of the team's other Latino stars provided the hitting heroics. Rico Carty, a heavy-hitting outfielder from the Dominican Republic, smashed his 15th home run of the season. Carty's sixth-inning blast tied the game at 2-2. Tony González, a center fielder from Cuba, delivered an RBI single in the seventh inning to break the tie. The Braves scored another run in the eighth to cap off a 4-2 victory, their eighth straight win. With the Giants losing to the Dodgers that evening, the Braves' lead increased to two and a half games.

The following afternoon, Cepeda again went hitless, but González chipped in with two more hits. Carty supplied another home run, a two-run shot that came in the first inning. The Braves never looked back, posting a 4-2 win, and earning Carty a post-game hug from Cepeda. The victory assured Atlanta of no less than a tie in the race to win the

Western Division. The Braves needed only one more win to clinch the West outright.

A capacity crowd of nearly 44,000 fans poured into Atlanta's Fulton County Stadium for Tuesday night's game against the Cincinnati Reds. For the third straight game, Cepeda went hitless. Once again it didn't matter. González went 4-for-4 and drove in the game-tying run in the bottom of the seventh. Two batters later, Carty lofted a sacrifice fly that scored Felix Millán from third. With future Hall of Famer Hoyt Wilhelm shutting down the Reds over the final two innings, the Braves won their tenth consecutive game and clinched the Western Division title.

Just as he had done with St. Louis and San Francisco, Cepeda took part in a victorious post-game celebration. As Carty tried to avoid the flow of champagne and beer by hiding under a table, Cepeda kept repeating one word over and over. "Beautiful, beautiful, beautiful," Cepeda shouted. That one word summed up Orlando's feelings about winning . . . and baseball.

When the Braves wrapped up the National League West, it brought to mind a statement that Cepeda had made time and time again. He had been asked repeatedly about the trade that had sent him from St. Louis to Atlanta. "The only thing that matters is who wins the pennant," Cepeda had answered. "That proves who won the deal." By that standard, the Braves had clearly won out. They had finished with the best record in the West, while the Cardinals had finished a disappointing fourth in the Eastern Division.

As champions of the Western Division, the Braves earned the right to play the New York Mets in the first National League Championship Series. The Mets had surprised the baseball world by overtaking the favored Chicago Cubs in September. The best-of-five playoff series would provide an interesting matchup: the intimidating, hard-throwing pitching staff of the Mets against the power-packed lineup of the Braves.

Two twenty-game winners faced each other in Game One. Atlanta's knuckleballing ace, Phil Niekro, had won twenty-three games during the regular season. New York's Tom Seaver, nicknamed "Tom Terrific," had won a league-leading twenty-five decisions. Yet, neither of these future Hall of Famers pitched up to his potential in the first game. The Braves scored five times against Seaver, taking a one-run lead to the top of the eighth.

With Niekro still on the mound, Wayne Garrett led off the eighth with a double. Cleon Jones quickly singled, scoring Garrett with the game-tying run. Art Shamsky followed with a third consecutive hit, sending Jones to second. When Ken Boswell missed on a bunt attempt, Atlanta catcher Bob Didier made a mistake and tried to pick off Jones at second. But the fleet-footed Jones wasn't trying to make it back to second; he had already begun racing for third, and made it safely. After Boswell bounced into a forceout, Ed Kranepool hit a ground ball toward first. Not wanting to give up the go-ahead run, Cepeda threw to the plate. Although Orlando made the right choice in trying to nab the runner at home, he executed the play poorly. His throw sailed past the catcher, who had no chance to make a play on the runner coming from third base. Jones scored on Cepeda's error, giving the Mets a 6-5 lead. The Mets went on to score three more times to win the first game, 9-5.

In Game Two, Cepeda did his best to make amends for the throwing error. He picked up two hits in four at-bats. His fifth-inning double helped the Braves put together a five-run rally.

Unfortunately for the Braves, their offense scraped out only two more hits the rest of the way. They couldn't catch up to the Mets, who had scored nine runs over the first five innings. The Mets went on to win the game, 11-6. The New

Yorkers needed just one more victory to advance to the World Series and eliminate the Braves from the playoffs.

With his team's season on the line, Cepeda enjoyed another good day at the plate in Game Three. He picked up two hits and two RBIs. His performance included a two-run homer against future Hall of Famer Nolan Ryan, giving the Braves a 4-3 lead.

Those two runs would be the only ones scored by the Braves against Ryan, who had entered the game in relief of starter Gary Gentry. Ryan held Atlanta down the rest of the way, while the Mets scored four runs against the Braves' battered pitching staff. A 7-4 final gave the Mets a sweep of the series and a berth in the World Series against the Baltimore Orioles.

The losses to the Mets provided some cruel irony for Cepeda. He had batted .455 in the series, the best batting average of any Braves' regular. He had driven in three runs and scored two runs. In terms of pure offense, it was the best post-season series of Cepeda's career. Yet, his team had lost—in three straight games. In 1967, the circumstances had reversed themselves. Cepeda had endured a nightmarish World Series at the plate, but his Cardinals had still managed to win the world championship. Orlando liked those circumstances much better than the current ones.

# Chapter Eleven

## Injured in Atlanta

Based on his performance during the first half of the 1970 season, Cepeda's second year in Atlanta seemed to be turning out even better than his first. He was hitting for a high average, while slamming home runs and driving in runs at his usual pace. In July, Cepeda enjoyed arguably his finest day in a major league uniform.

The Braves played the Cubs in a doubleheader at Wrigley Field. Orlando had always enjoyed hitting at Wrigley, with its short distances to the power alleys. This day would prove to be no different. Cepeda hit three home runs in the first game, including a grand slam. It marked the first time he had gone deep that many times in a single game. Each time he victimized right-hander Bill Hands, a pitcher who liked to throw curveballs. "I usually hit him good," Cepeda told sportswriter Pete Coutros of the *New York Post* many years later. "That was because I liked that curve on the outside; I could hit that one a lot better than a fastball."

Cepeda piled up seven RBIs in the first game. He didn't fare too badly in the second game, either, picking up three hits in four at-bats. That gave him a doubleheader total of seven hits in nine at-bats. If only Orlando could have played his entire career at Wrigley Field!

By season's end, Orlando had put up some of the best numbers of his career. He finished the season with a .305 batting average, the first time he had reached .300 since 1967. He also totaled 34 home runs and 111 RBIs. In spite of all the individual success, however, 1970 left several scars with Orlando. One involved the Braves' failure to win the pennant. They finished behind the Cincinnati Reds, who captured the National League West.

Another scar, which was caused by marital problems, was worse. Orlando and his wife separated in 1970. Ana had discovered that Orlando was again unfaithful to her, something that had happened several times during their marriage. Ana told Orlando to leave their house; three years later, they would officially finalize their divorce.

And then there were scars of bigotry. During the season, several racists confronted Cepeda's four-year-old son, Orlando Xavier. "They called him a nigger, a Puerto Rican monkey," Cepeda recalled for *Black Sports Magazine*. "He had never heard these words before. I had to explain to him what they meant when they called him nigger. It was not easy." Although Cepeda generally liked Atlanta, that group of racist fans reminded him of the disturbing atmosphere he had seen in the Braves' clubhouse. Black, white, and Latin players on the team did not get along that well. There were obvious tensions between the three ethnic groups. The atmosphere was a lot different than the racial harmony that Cepeda had experienced during his days with the Cardinals.

Although Orlando had put forth an outstanding performance in 1970, Atlanta decided to offer him in trades to other teams. The Braves needed help on the mound, and felt a great hitter like Cepeda could bring them a quality pitcher in return. One rumor had Cepeda heading to the Chicago Cubs for outfielder Johnny Callison and a pitcher. Another report had Cepeda going to the Kansas City Royals for a promising young pitcher named Marty Pattin.

The trade rumors didn't upset a veteran player like Cepeda, who remained with the Braves heading into the 1971 season. "They didn't bother me at all. No matter where I play, I have to do my job," Orlando told Wayne Minshew of *The Sporting News.* "Life is too short to worry about small things." Especially things that Cepeda couldn't control.

Cepeda did have control over his hitting, which was as good as it had ever been. By the start of June, Cepeda had piled up 14 home runs and 44 RBIs. He was on pace to put together his finest power season ever. And then came the late-night telephone call.

As he was tape-recording some music, Orlando heard the phone ring. It would not turn out to be an urgent phone call. But as Cepeda lifted himself up to answer the phone, his left knee collapsed underneath his weight. The knee swelled up, causing him pain. He tried to keep playing, but the pain and inflammation became too much to bear. On August 13, he underwent a two-hour, season-ending operation to remove cartilage and repair a stretched ligament in the bad knee. For the first time since 1965, Cepeda would not be able to play a full major league season.

Orlando strengthened the knee by lifting weights and running on the beach, something that was tough to do because of the way sand gives out under one's legs. Once he felt strong enough, he played about twenty-five games in the Puerto Rican Winter League in the hopes that it would help him get ready for the 1972 campaign. He felt optimistic that he would be able to play regularly, especially since this latest knee injury had not been as serious as the problems he had endured in 1965.

Spring training arrived, but the Braves kept Cepeda out of the early exhibition games. They wanted him to take it easy in his comeback. They also wanted their team doctor to keep a close eye on his left knee. From time to time, the doctor had to drain the knee. He did that by inserting a sharp needle, which removed excess fluid that had built up in the knee.

By the middle of March, when Cepeda played in his first spring training game, the knee had already been drained four times. He went 0-for-3 in his debut, but hit two balls fairly hard in the Braves' 1-0 win over the New York Yankees. After the game, he placed a cold pack of ice on his left knee. He held it there for ten minutes, until the knee felt numb.

He repeated the process after each game he played. He also lifted weights with his left leg. He played some games, but sat out other ones. The knee felt good some days, but hurt on other days. "That is the way it is with a knee," Orlando told Ron Hudspeth of the *Atlanta Journal.* "You can never tell about tomorrow."

The Braves didn't know what the future held for Cepeda. They worried about his ability to last a full season without re-injuring the knee. The Braves faced another dilemma, too. The team's longtime star, Hank Aaron, wanted to play first base. He had played well there after Cepeda's season-ending surgery in 1971. Aaron also thought his career would last longer if he played first base, an easier position than his usual spot in the outfield.

If Aaron moved to first, Cepeda would have no place to play. He couldn't play the outfield anymore, not like he had for the Giants earlier in his career. As a result, the Braves started talking with other teams about possible trades. One team, the New York Mets, badly wanted a hitter of Cepeda's ability. One rumor had the Mets offering the Braves young fireballer Nolan Ryan, who would one day make the Hall of Fame. According to another rumor, the Mets offered one of their older pitchers for Cepeda. Ironically, it was Ray Sadecki, the same player that had been traded for Cepeda once before. The Braves said no; they wanted both Sadecki and a young pitcher, Jim McAndrew. New York's manager, Gil Hodges, didn't like that idea at all. A few days later, Cepeda hit a game-winning home run against the Mets, but Hodges still wouldn't budge on New York's offer to the Braves.

The trade talk soon came to an end, interrupted by labor problems between the major league players and the owners. The players left spring training, having decided to go out on strike. That was bad news for Orlando, who would not be allowed to work out under the supervision of the Braves or their team doctor. If he wanted to continue working out, he would have to take a chance and do it on his own. Otherwise, he might fall out of shape and find himself behind the other players when the strike came to an end.

Sure enough, Orlando twisted his knee while working out in Puerto Rico. When the strike ended and Opening Day rolled around, Cepeda tried to return to the Braves' lineup right away. He came to bat only once before aggravating the knee. Manager Luman Harris removed him from the game, substituting Dusty Baker as a pinch-hitter. Cepeda returned to the clubhouse, where the team doctor drained his knee with a needle.

Cepeda said he wanted to play badly, but the knee simply hurt too much. Feeling like he had hit rock-bottom, Orlando talked about making a change in careers. "I may quit [baseball]," Cepeda informed the *Atlanta Journal.* "I am serious. The pain and the needles are getting to be too much. I don't want to go through any more pain."

A doctor specializing in knee injuries asked Cepeda to try a special weightlifting program. Desperate for a remedy to his pain, Cepeda agreed to do it for at least a couple of weeks. If his knee didn't feel better by then, he would officially announce his retirement.

The knee wasn't the only thing causing him pain. Some members of the Braves' organization began to question whether he was really hurt. Cepeda overheard some of the people who doubted his injury, saying he didn't want to earn his $90,000-per-year paycheck. "I'm making a big salary so they think I can play but [that] I don't want to," Cepeda told the *New York Times.* And who was making these accusations?

"Like the coaches," Orlando revealed. "They see a guy making big money and they say, 'Look at this guy. He's Latin, he's making big money and he could be playing.'" Orlando had heard the same criticism during his years in San Francisco. In some ways, the negative stereotypes of Latin American players hadn't changed.

As Orlando continued to hear from his doubters, his knee actually started to feel better. The doctor's last-ditch weight program seemed to be working. Cepeda felt good enough to return to the Braves' lineup on April 30. He felt even better after his at-bat in the second inning, when he ripped a home run into the left-field stands. The blast gave the Braves their first run on the way to a 6-1 rout of the Pittsburgh Pirates.

Cepeda played regularly for the next three weeks, even hitting two home runs in one game. Then the left knee started bothering him again. He went back to the bench before the Braves ordered him to return to Atlanta for more treatment. *Here we go again,* Cepeda must have thought.

Cepeda's knee eventually felt better, but he remained on the bench most of the time. In June, Cepeda received a start in a Friday-night game against the Montreal Expos. He batted seventh—the lowest he had ever hit in the major leagues—and picked up two hits. Cepeda felt good. The knee was not 100 percent, but it was good enough for him to play regularly. More importantly, he believed that he had worked his way back into the starting lineup.

Not so fast. Luman Harris decided not to play him the next day. Orlando couldn't understand why. As the Associated Press explained it, he went to Harris and asked him about being benched again. "I'm the manager," Harris told Cepeda bluntly, "and I think the club is stronger with the lineup I wrote."

Those words hurt Cepeda. According to the Associated Press, Cepeda gave Harris an angry reply. "Trade me, release me, or give me away." Cepeda had one other announcement to make. "I'm going home." With the game against the Expos scheduled to start in less than a few hours, Cepeda packed up his bags and left Atlanta's Fulton County Stadium. He was leaving the team.

A reporter from the Associated Press called Cepeda the next day and asked him why he had left the team so suddenly. "I'm fed up with not playing," Orlando answered. "They treat me like garbage."

Why had Harris decided to bench Cepeda, who claimed he was now healthy? After all, Orlando was hitting over .300 in part-time duty and had picked up two hits on Friday night. In one sense, Cepeda had lost his first base job to the legendary Hank Aaron, who would soon become the game's all-time home run king. But in another sense, Cepeda had lost out to one of the team's younger players. Harris wanted to make room in the lineup for a promising outfielder named Mike Lum. By moving Aaron from the outfield to first base, the Braves could create a spot for Lum to play regularly. Cepeda became the odd man out.

Whatever the Braves' thinking, Cepeda had made a mistake by walking out on the team. Although Orlando had reason to be frustrated over a lack of playing time, he could have handled the situation in a different way. Instead of abandoning the team in the middle of the season, he could have asked to meet with his manager in private. Or he could have vowed to make himself the best pinch-hitter in the National League until he somehow made it back into the regular lineup. Upset and confused, Cepeda took the wrong route.

The Braves responded to Cepeda's walkout in two different ways. Luman Harris suspended him indefinitely. And team vice-president Paul Richards said he would do his best to accommodate him and trade him to another team.

Orlando had asked Atlanta to do one of three things: trade him, release him, or give him away. If the Braves released him, they would receive nothing in return for an excellent major league hitter. They didn't want that. Instead, the Braves sought to make a trade with another team. That way, the Braves would receive a player or money—something—in exchange for the talented Cepeda.

Atlanta needed to find Cepeda a new team, one that would be willing to pay his large $90,000 salary. The new team would also have to be willing to take a chance on a player who had walked out on his current team.

It would be easier to find Cepeda a new team if he first came back to the Braves. On June 19, two days after he had walked out, Cepeda met with Luman Harris and Eddie Robinson, the team's director of player personnel. Orlando agreed to return the team. Harris and Robinson agreed to reinstate him from the suspended list. Although the Braves made no announcement, they also docked Cepeda two days' pay.

Ten days later, the Braves finally found a taker for Cepeda. They struck a deal with the Oakland A's, who were looking to trade one of their own high-priced players. The A's decided to buy Cepeda from the Braves; in return, Atlanta agreed to purchase veteran pitcher Denny McLain, a former star who had been troubled by gambling and weight problems in recent years. It was basically a trade of superstars, the first time that onetime league Most Valuable Players had been traded for one another. The Braves hoped that McLain would regain the form that had made him a thirty-one-game winner for the Detroit Tigers in 1968. In turn, the A's hoped that Cepeda would be able to share playing time with the left-handed hitting Mike Epstein at first base.

For Cepeda, the sale to Oakland allowed him to return for the Bay Area, where he had last played six years earlier for the San Francisco Giants. "I am always happy," Orlando told a reporter who asked him if he was pleased about joining the A's. "Only when I do not play am I unhappy." Although upset about his lack of playing time in Atlanta, he refused to criticize his former bosses. "I don't want to be like some other players who knock the club when they leave," Orlando told the Associated Press. "[The Braves] were good to me. They took care of me last year when my knee had to be operated on." It was a classy response from Cepeda, who simply hoped for a fresh start in Oakland.

Questions remained about Cepeda's health. "My only concern is my knee," he told the Associated Press. If Cepeda's left knee could hold up, he could help the A's in their quest to repeat as champions of the American League West.

That was Cepeda's hope, but it proved to be wishful thinking. In reality, Cepeda's left knee was now worse than ever. His knee had become so bad that he could hardly stand up without feeling pain in his leg. The same man who had stolen 23 bases in 1959—the same man who was clocked the fastest of all the Giants in 1958—could barely run from home to first. Oakland manager Dick Williams wanted to start Cepeda against left-handed pitchers, but the condition of Orlando's leg would not allow it. Orlando came to bat three times as a pinch-hitter—without getting a base hit. The A's soon realized that Cepeda was not healthy enough to play at all. He would have to undergo surgery— yet again. Cepeda would miss the rest of the 1972 season.

Cepeda traveled with the team on a couple of road trips. He watched his new teammates—outstanding players like Bert "Campy" Campaneris, Rollie Fingers, Catfish Hunter, and Reggie Jackson—lead the A's to the first of three consecutive appearances in the World Series. But Orlando could not participate. As the A's played the Cincinnati Reds in the World Series, Cepeda lifted weights in the Marines Memorial Club in San Francisco. As he tried to strengthen his knee, he did not feel like he was an important part of the team, like he had been in San Francisco and St. Louis, or even Atlanta. After the A's beat the Reds in seven games, Cepeda did not even receive a World Series ring.

Cepeda also worried about his future. Would he remain with the A's, or he would he be sent off to another team? Given the condition of his knees, would it even matter? At thirty-five years old, Cepeda wondered whether he would be able to play major league baseball again.

# Chapter Twelve

# Saved by a Rule

As the A's celebrated their World Series triumph, Cepeda continued to ponder his fate in baseball. His situation in Oakland started to clarify in late November, when the A's traded starting first baseman Mike Epstein to the Texas Rangers. Team owner Charlie Finley announced that Gene Tenace, the hero of the World Series, would move from catcher to first base. Now, if the left-handed hitting Epstein had remained on the team, the A's could have played him against right-handed pitchers, and Cepeda against left-handers. Since Tenace batted right-handed—just like Orlando—there seemed to be no role for Cepeda with the A's.

On December 18, the A's did the expected when they gave Cepeda his unconditional release. After checking with the team physician, Charlie Finley concluded that Cepeda could no longer run well enough to play professionally. Orlando saw it differently, however. He believed that Finley had decided to release him because of his large salary. By releasing him during the winter, Finley owed Cepeda no more money.

Still, Cepeda felt no anger or surprise over the decision; after all, he didn't want to play for Finley. He considered the A's owner a difficult boss. "I was happy [about being released]," Cepeda told the *New York Times*. "I never liked Oakland." Yet, Orlando was now out of a job—perhaps for good.

If other teams believed what Finley had said, they wouldn't take a chance on Cepeda. What good was a player who couldn't run? A pitcher, perhaps, might be able to get away with that, but not a player who had to run the bases regularly and move around the infield defensively.

Just when it appeared that Cepeda's career had hit a permanent snag, the American League announced that it would introduce a new rule in 1973. Each team would be able to use a "designated hitter," who would bat in place of the pitcher. The designated hitter—known as the DH—would not have to play in the field, like a shortstop or a catcher or a center fielder. All he had to do was take his turn in the batting order.

By bringing in the DH, the American League hoped to add more offense—and excitement—to the game. The rule seemed to be made for players like Cepeda, veteran stars who could still hit, but were too old or fragile to play a position in the field.

The rule also seemed perfect for Minnesota Twins' star Pedro "Tony" Oliva, an older player with bad knees of his own and one of Cepeda's best friends in baseball. "The day they make the rule, I was on the phone asking Tony how he was feeling," Cepeda told the *New York Times*. "He told me about this new rule and told me to sign with [the] Boston [Red Sox]. He said they have a great organization. The Texas Rangers and the [Chicago] White Sox also wanted me." Orlando listened carefully to Oliva's advice.

Cepeda also received phone calls from the New York Mets and Pittsburgh Pirates, two National League teams that wouldn't be able to use the DH. But Orlando had made up his mind. He wanted to play for the team that Ted Williams, his hitting hero, had helped make famous. Orlando remembered the first baseball game he had ever seen on television—the 1950 All-Star Game, which featured Williams in his prime. He also recalled the day in 1959 when he had watched the Boston Red Sox's star take spring training batting practice in Phoenix, Arizona. He had looked on in amazement as Williams unleashed his beautiful swing, sending line drive after line drive into the outfield. Orlando had become a fan of the man considered the greatest hitter who ever lived.

A few days after the designated hitter rule became official, the Boston Red Sox announced that they had signed Cepeda to become their first DH. He would take a paycut from his previous salary, but would still make about $80,000 for the upcoming season. Orlando was now ready to start his "second" career in baseball.

# Chapter Thirteen

# The Beantown Basher

Although Orlando was excited about his second chance in baseball, he was also saddened by some terrible news that he heard at the start of 1973. Another great player from Puerto Rico, someone that Cepeda knew well, had been killed in a plane crash on New Year's Eve. It was Roberto Clemente, someone that Orlando had first met when he was only seventeen years old. In fact, Clemente had taken care of Orlando and four other Puerto Rican prospects when they made their first trip to the mainland. "I was on the plane with him back in 1955 when I first came to the United States to play baseball," Cepeda told Fred Ciampa of the *Boston Herald*. "Roberto was a wonderful, wonderful fellow." With Clemente gone, Cepeda was now the most famous athlete from Puerto Rico still playing in the major leagues.

Yet, Cepeda had almost been forgotten as a major league ballplayer. During the winter, his seven-year-old son had picked up a pre-season baseball magazine, which previewed all twenty-four major league teams. Orlando Xavier looked through the entire magazine, but couldn't find his father's name. "The magazine was supposed to be about all the people in the major leagues," the elder Cepeda mentioned to a sportswriter from the *Post-Dispatch*, "and my name wasn't even in it." The magazine had given up on Cepeda's career; fortunately, Orlando and the Red Sox had not.

In the meantime, some followers of baseball began criticizing the new designated hitter rule that had given Orlando the opportunity to continue his career. One of the critics was longtime American League star Frank Robinson, who was now playing with the California Angels. Robinson claimed that any player who did not play in the field was not a complete player. Cepeda respectfully disagreed with Robinson's point. "To me, hitting *is* baseball," he argued in an interview with Mark Twersky of the *New York Times.* "If you hit, you're a good player. If you can't hit, you're nothing. I am a complete baseball player."

But also a slow one. Cepeda ran so slowly that some baseball writers joked about it. Dick Young of the *New York Daily News* wrote that the Red Sox would need a designated *runner* for Cepeda every time he reached base. Of course, there was no such player allowed in baseball.

Orlando's teammates also teased him. "If they put in the designated pinch-runner rule," shortstop Luis Aparicio shouted to Cepeda, "I don't think you will get the job." Cepeda took the needling in stride. He reminded Aparicio, a nine-time American League stolen base king, that he no longer ran that well, either. After all, Luis had only stolen three bases the previous year.

Cepeda no longer had much speed on the bases, but he felt confident about another aspect of his game. When a reporter from United Press International asked him if his career might be nearly over, Orlando offered an interesting answer. "I don't know," he responded honestly. "Even if I am [finished] as a player, I can still hit. I'm a better hitter now than I ever was."

In spite of his self-confidence at the plate, Orlando's new baseball life in Boston did not begin well. He went hitless in his first two regular season games. Having gone without a hit in his first 11 at-bats, Cepeda came to bat in the ninth inning of the season's third game. He faced New York Yankee left-hander Sparky Lyle, one of the best relievers in the American League and the owner of a devastating slider.

The slump soon ended. Cepeda blasted one of Lyle's trade-mark sliders for a home run, winning the game dramatically for the Red Sox.

The home run lifted Cepeda's spirits—and his hitting. He went on a tear at the plate. In his first sixty-one games of the season, he collected 11 home runs and 37 RBIs. He was on pace to hit close to 30 home runs and drive in nearly 100 runs.

Cepeda also lifted weights as part of a program to strengthen his knees and legs. His knees felt so much better that he talked about playing first base again. He hadn't done that since playing the infield for the Braves at the start of the 1972 season.

The Red Sox really didn't care if Cepeda could play first base. They wanted him simply for his ability to swing the bat. As long as he could run the bases without getting hurt, the Sox would be happy.

Although Cepeda could no longer run well, he was at least running faster than he had for the A's a year ago. He was also running the bases smartly. In early August, Cepeda ran out four doubles in a game against the Kansas City Royals. The quartet of doubles tied a major league record. With six RBIs, Cepeda led the Red Sox to a 9-4 win over the Royals.

He continued to hit so well that he ended up becoming arguably the American League's most productive DH. He finished the season with 20 home runs for the Red Sox—marking the fourth team for which he had reached the single-season milestone. Only one other designated hitter produced more home runs than Cepeda during the first year of the new rule. Only one other DH collected more RBIs. The American League rewarded him by voting him Designated Hitter of the Year. Orlando Cepeda had given the Red Sox just the kind of power that they had been wanting from baseball's new "10th man."

# Chapter Fourteen

# Last Stop, Kansas City

Cepeda had enjoyed his first season in Boston. He especially liked Eddie Kasko, the Red Sox's manager. In fact, Orlando liked Kasko so much that he considered him one of his favorite major league managers.

So when the Red Sox fired Kasko after the 1973 season, Cepeda felt crushed. He would now have to play for Darrell Johnson, Kasko's replacement. For Orlando, the change in managers was a sign of bad things to come.

Based on his first season in Boston, it seemed like Cepeda had little reason to worry about his job during spring training in 1974. As one of the best designated hitters in the league, Cepeda gave the Red Sox a commodity that they always needed: right-handed power. Plus, he seemed to be running better than he had in 1973. Given all of that, his job seemed safe in Boston. At least that seemed to be the case.

On March 26, the Red Sox delivered a surprise announcement to the media. They told reporters that they had decided to release three well-known veteran players. One was thirty-five-year-old reliever Bobby Bolin, the team's best relief pitcher in 1973 and one of Cepeda's teammates during his days in San Francisco. Another was thirty-nine-year-old shortstop Luis Aparicio, one of Venezuela's greatest players and a future Hall of Famer. And the third player? Unbelievably, it was Cepeda, who had been one of Boston's best power hitters in 1973. And it wasn't like Orlando was struggling during spring training. He had hit .313 with five RBIs in four exhibition games. The decision to release Cepeda didn't seem to make sense.

Some of the Boston writers said that the Red Sox wanted to get rid of Cepeda because of his poor running speed. They felt he clogged up the basepaths. Of course, Cepeda moved a lot of runners *off* the basepaths by hitting home runs, too.

Manager Darrell Johnson explained that he now had other hitters who could perform the DH role that Cepeda had filled. He mentioned players like Bernie Carbo, Cecil Cooper, and Dick McAuliffe. Yet, Carbo was inconsistent, Cooper was unproven, and McAuliffe had never been as dangerous a hitter as Cepeda. So what was Johnson thinking?

Cepeda had his own theory. "It was a personal thing," Orlando told Peter Gammons of *The Sporting News.* "He [Johnson] doesn't like me." One week earlier, Cepeda said that Johnson had told him he was going to remain the team's everyday designated hitter. Cepeda said that Johnson had assured him of that—twice. And then Johnson decided to release him. "He is two-faced," Cepeda said, describing the Red Sox's manager. If only Eddie Kasko had kept his job, Cepeda might have, too.

Johnson denied ever having promised Cepeda the DH role. Still, one question remained unanswered. Why didn't the Red Sox try to trade Cepeda to another team and get something of value in return? Apparently, the Red Sox didn't care. They just wanted to get rid of Cepeda's big contract, along with the salaries of Aparicio and Bolin. That way the Red Sox could replace them on the roster with younger, cheaper players.

Weren't there any other American League teams that could have used a DH like "The Baby Bull?" The Kansas City Royals needed a power hitter and thought about signing Cepeda. Royals' manager Jack McKeon wanted the veteran slugger to be his designated hitter. Cedric Tallis, Kansas City's general manager and McKeon's boss, preferred a younger player named Hal McRae to be the team's DH. Tallis won out, leaving Cepeda out of a job.

Three other teams expressed interest in Cepeda, but none of them offered him a contract. "I was surprised that nobody else wanted me," Cepeda told Robert Moore of the Associated Press. "I talked to the New York Yankees, Cleveland Indians, and the Chicago White Sox, but I guess they thought I was making too much money."

After two and a half months without a major league offer, Orlando finally decided to sign with a team in the Mexican League. On June 15, he agreed to play for Yucatan. Although the quality of play in the Mexican League was good, it was nowhere near the level of play in the major leagues. It would have to do for now, at least until a big league club showed some interest in the thirty-five-year-old slugger.

Cepeda played well for Yucatan. The Royals, along with some other American League teams, sent scouts to watch Cepeda play. If the scouts came away impressed, they might recommend signing Cepeda to play for their team.

One of those American League teams finally gave Cepeda a call in July. It was the Royals, who still needed a power hitter and a DH. They figured Cepeda would join them quickly. Not so. Orlando told the Royals he couldn't sign with them—at least not right away. He didn't want to abandon Yucatan, which was battling for a spot in the Mexican League playoffs. He felt it was important to remain loyal to a team that had given him a chance to play when no one else showed interest. Dick Young, the famed baseball writer with the *New York Daily News,* applauded Orlando for being a "man of honor."

Three weeks later, Yucatan failed to make the playoffs. The Royals, perhaps appreciating Cepeda's loyalty to his team, still wanted to sign him. They were impressed by his play with Yucatan, where he had banged out four home runs and 16 RBIs in only 70 at-bats. The Royals agreed to pay Cepeda $30,000 to be their designated hitter for the rest of the season.

Why did the Royals change their mind about adding Cepeda, whom they had decided not to sign at the end of spring training? First, Cedric Tallis was no longer the Royals' general manager, having been replaced in mid-season by Joe Burke. Second, the Royals needed a veteran hitter to help them catch the first-place Oakland A's. So when manager Jack McKeon asked his new boss about signing Cepeda, Burke agreed that it was a good move.

"He gives us added depth, another big bat, and a psychological lift," McKeon told Sid Bordman of *The Sporting News*. "You look at most of the pennant winners in past years, and they picked up a big bat for the stretch." McKeon was right. In 1972, the Oakland A's had traded for veteran Dominican outfielder Matty Alou. Cepeda's former teammate in San Francisco batted .281 down the stretch, helping the A's win the American League West. In 1973, the A's added two other Latino batsmen—Jesus Alou and Vic Davalillo—who delivered several key hits during the playoffs. Alou and Davalillo helped the A's win their second consecutive world championship.

The other Royals' players hoped that Cepeda would bring similar results to Kansas City. They respected what Cepeda had done in the past, for teams like the Cardinals and Braves. They looked at the signing of Cepeda as a sign that the front office had not given up on Kansas City's season. The Royals trailed the A's by eight games, which was not an impossible difference to overcome. Perhaps the Royals could still catch the A's after all.

The decision to sign Cepeda looked even better when John Mayberry, the team's top power hitter, broke his right hand a few days later. With Mayberry out indefinitely, the Royals needed a power hitter like Cepeda that much more.

McKeon made room for Cepeda in his lineup by moving Hal McRae from DH to left field. The Royals responded well to the change. In Cepeda's first game, Kansas City picked up 20 hits and beat the Minnesota Twins, 17-3. Cepeda went 2-for-4, driving in a pair of runs with a single. A few days later, Cepeda pounded out two doubles and drove in five runs to help the Royals beat the Milwaukee Brewers, 13-3. In only five games with the Royals, Cepeda had driven in 10 runs—or an average of two RBIs a game. The Royals had won four of the five games.

The other players on the Royals appreciated what Cepeda was bringing to the team. "That's the man who is doing it," Hal McRae told Sid Bordman of *The Sporting News.* "He's got us going." Jack McKeon was just as happy with his new acquisition. "We weren't getting the big hits, and this guy comes along and shows us how," the manager told *The Sporting News.*

In particular, Cepeda was showing one of the team's best young players how to hit. Rookie infielder George Brett was considered one of the brightest prospects in the brief six-year history of the Royals' franchise. He played third base brilliantly, ranging far to his left and right in snapping up ground balls. He also ran the bases with speed and daring. And he had a beautiful line-drive swing.

The Royals loved Brett's enormous potential, but grew concerned over his continuing struggles at the plate. Prior to Cepeda's arrival in the lineup, Brett's batting average stood at only .236. His daily work with batting coach Charlie Lau didn't seem to be paying immediate dividends.

Once Cepeda joined the Royals, Brett's bat came to life. From the day that Cepeda made his Royals' debut until the end of the season, Brett improved his average to .282. That was an increase of 46 points.

Was it just a coincidence that Brett's batting improved after Cepeda joined the team? Perhaps not. Cepeda usually batted fifth in the order, with Brett taking his turn as the seventh-or eighth-place hitter. Such a batting order allowed Brett to watch Cepeda from the dugout. He could study how Cepeda approached each of his at-bats. Brett could discover some real insights about hitting by observing one of the veterans of the game.

It was a classic case of the student watching the master. A young player on his way up, trying to prove himself at the major league level, and an aging veteran nearing the end of a great career.

Although Cepeda played only part of the season with the Royals, he had a feeling about Brett's future greatness. "Oh yeah," Cepeda says with emphasis. "You could tell, he was a gamer." Twenty-five years later, Brett would enter the Hall of Fame as one of the finest-hitting third basemen in the history of the game.

In the meantime, manager Jack McKeon had just one regret about Cepeda: not signing him earlier in the season. "Just think if we would have had him since May 1," McKeon told *The Sporting News.* "We'd be fifteen games over .500."

As it was, the Royals had put together a win-loss record just two games over .500 by the time Cepeda made his Kansas City debut. With six wins in Cepeda's first seven games with the team, the Royals improved their record to 60-53.

Then, without warning, the Royals started to struggle. During the rest of August, they won only nine of nineteen games. As the season headed into September, they suffered through a brutal eight-game losing streak, followed quickly by a seven-game skid. The Royals didn't make the playoffs. They completely collapsed in September, losing twenty of twenty-eight games. They finished thirteeen games back of the Oakland A's in the Western Division race.

Cepeda began slumping at about the same time that the Royals did. After his hot start, his hitting fell off drastically. He ended the season with a .215 batting average, the second worst of his career. He hit only one home run as a Royal, matching his career low for a season.

After the season, the Royals announced that they had given Orlando his unconditional release. Once again, Cepeda's future in baseball was in real jeopardy.

No other major league team showed interest in the aging designated hitter. Only one team—a club in the Japanese League—made him an offer. The contract was a good one, paying him $250,000 for one season. Cepeda had never earned that much money during his best days in the major leagues.

Orlando thought about the offer. The money was great, but the Japanese League was a step down in quality from the major leagues. Playing in the Far East, he would also have to adjust to a completely different language and culture. Cepeda thought carefully about the offer, and then turned it down. He then made another decision. At thirty-seven years of age, Orlando Cepeda decided to retire from the sport he had played professionally since the mid-1950s.

# Chapter Fifteen

# Trouble with the Law

For the first time since 1955, Orlando Cepeda would not be playing professional baseball in the United States. He announced that he would spend most of his time on the construction of a gymnasium, a kind of health spa, in his native Puerto Rico. He also began making a number of trips to Colombia, where he was conducting baseball clinics.

On December 12, Orlando called one of his friends, former minor league player Herminio Cortes, to see if he had picked up two suitcases and two cartons that were waiting for him at San Juan's Isla Verde International Airport. Cepeda had arranged for the four pieces of luggage to be sent to him on a flight from Colombia, from where he had just returned. When Orlando discovered that Cortes had not picked up the packages as promised, he decided to drive to the airport. Orlando would claim the packages himself.

As Orlando prepared to carry the cartons and suitcases to his car—a red Mercedes that was parked outside of the airport terminal—federal drug agents confronted him. The drug agents had been investigating Cepeda, suspicious over his repeated trips to Colombia. They had been keeping him under surveillance for the past few days.

Looking inside the cartons, the drug agents found some new cowhide rugs. That wasn't all that they noticed. They found plastic bags filled with marijuana, which were strapped to the rugs. Reports varied on the amount of marijuana found, anywhere from 60 to 160 pounds, with a monetary worth estimated as high as $60,000. The agents arrested Cepeda, charging him with possession and importing of illegal drugs.

Cepeda claimed that he didn't know about the marijuana. He said that during his most recent visit to Colombia he had noticed the cowhide rugs and had asked to have a few of them sent to him. Cepeda said that the man who sent him the rugs had placed the drugs in the cartons without telling him. He contended that he had been "tricked" into picking up the cartons. Orlando insisted that he was innocent, the victim of a set-up.

The federal drug agents didn't believe Cepeda. They accused him of buying the red Mercedes with money he had raised from selling drugs. Cepeda insisted that wasn't the case. He explained that the Boston Red Sox had given him the car as a bonus when he signed with them in 1973.

News of Cepeda's arrest spread quickly throughout Puerto Rico. Even though the charges against him had not yet been brought to trial, many Puerto Ricans felt angered and betrayed. They wondered how one of their baseball heroes could involve himself with drugs. How could the son of Perucho Cepeda, one of the island's most beloved figures, do something like this to disgrace the family name?

As a result of the arrest, Orlando became an outcast. "People were afraid to talk to me. They said I was Mafia," Cepeda told David Israel of the *Chicago Tribune* several years later. "They used to have pictures of me at the ballparks in Puerto Rico, but they take them away. The people say I'm a bad example to my boy and to their boys."

Cepeda heard the criticisms and the insults, and so did his family. In public, some friends of the family started to ignore Orlando's second wife, Nydia. Other people taunted her with nasty remarks. Still others telephoned Orlando's mother, saying that her son was the "shame of Puerto Rico." In the minds of many, Cepeda was already guilty.

The case against Cepeda eventually went to federal district court in San Juan. Judge Hernan Pasquera listened to the evidence brought forth by the drug agents and the testimony of witnesses, including Cepeda. On December 16, 1976, Judge Pasquera delivered his ruling. The judge believed that the drug agents had been justified in making the arrests. He convicted Cepeda of drug possession and drug smuggling, and fined him $10,000. But that wasn't the worst of it. The judge also sentenced Cepeda to five years in federal prison. Two years after his career as a major league player had come to an end, his life as a free man was also about to come to an end.

Cepeda first decided to fight the decision. He filed an appeal of the guilty verdict. While he waited for the appeal, he took a job as manager of an amateur team in Puerto Rico. He talked about eventually becoming a manager in the major leagues.

Those dreams were cut down when the appeal was turned aside. Cepeda filed another appeal, but it met with the same fate. The courts ordered Cepeda to surrender himself to federal marshals. On June 26, 1978, Orlando Cepeda entered the federal prison located at Eglin Air Force Base in Fort Walton Beach, Florida.

Unlike "maximum security" prisons, Eglin had no fences or walls. There were no jail cells. The grounds of the prison had well-maintained lawns and neatly trimmed hedges, making it look more like a college campus. The prison complex included a softball field, a basketball court, and tennis courts. All of these facilities were available to the prisoners.

But it was still prison. Almost every part of Orlando's day would be controlled and regulated by the guards and officers who worked there. Most importantly, Orlando was not free to come and go as he pleased. He was now an inmate. Prisoner No. 0700-155A.

In his first ten days at Eglin, Cepeda had to go through an orientation period. He had to clean dirty toilets and bathrooms, mop up soiled floors, and throw out garbage. During his first two weeks in prison, he cried every day.

After orientation, Orlando tried to find some activities to keep busy. He took a job working in the laundry room. He also worked as a translator, helping Spanish-speaking inmates communicate with prison officials. He lifted weights. And even though he was now forty years old, he decided to try out for the prison softball team. "I never played softball before, only baseball," Cepeda told the Associated Press. As a youngster, Orlando had once tried to play softball—which featured a larger ball and slower pitching—but his father pulled him from the playing field. Perucho didn't want his son playing a game that might hurt his skills in baseball. "This softball," Orlando admitted out loud, "I don't know if I can hit it."

More importantly, Cepeda decided to use his time in prison as a learning experience, "the greatest experience any man can have." In an interview with the Associated Press, he expressed an upbeat attitude. "I'm not bitter," Orlando said. "I thank God this has happened to me. Sometimes people don't see reality . . . Well, now I have seen reality. Here nobody is privileged. Everybody is equal. There are lawyers, doctors, bankers, judges, geniuses in all kinds of fields." In other words, anybody was capable of making mistakes, doing the wrong thing, regardless of their status in society.

During his stay at Eglin, Orlando came to another important realization. Although he had continued to insist that he had been "set up," he finally confessed to his knowledge of the drugs, which he had agreed to enclose in the packages as a favor to a friend. "I made a mistake," Cepeda admitted in an interview with the *Miami News*.

Cepeda did disagree with law enforcement officials about the amount of marijuana found in the packages. The drug agents claimed they had found about 160 pounds of the illegal drugs. Orlando argued that he had put only five pounds of marijuana in the packages. Whatever the case, Cepeda eventually explained how he had begun to use marijuana on a regular basis during his days with the Giants in the mid-1960s, and how he had used drugs during his last visit to Colombia before the arrest. During a cab ride, the driver had informed Cepeda that he could supply him with some "good stuff," or marijuana. Giving in to his own weakness, Orlando accepted the cab driver's offer. "Back then, I was having trouble coping without baseball," he explained to Ron Fimrite of *Sports Illustrated.* "I guess I had too much time on my hands."

Realizing the mistakes he had made, Cepeda behaved like a model prisoner during his stay at Eglin. He didn't complain or cause trouble. He performed his daily duties with an enthusiastic attitude.

Cepeda's good behavior played a part in earning him early release from prison. He ended up serving only ten months of his five-year sentence before being released on parole in April of 1979. By reentering the free world, the one without prison bars, Orlando would receive a second chance on his life.

Although Cepeda had regained his freedom, he had lost all of his money. He had spent about $300,000 paying off the legal fees for his trial. He even had to sell some of the baseball trophies and awards that he had won to pay off his debts. "I have only myself to blame," Orlando told *Sports Illustrated.* "Whatever happened to me was my fault, but I lost everything—car, home. My wife, Nydia, had to go on welfare." More importantly, Orlando had lost the respect of many of his fellow Puerto Ricans. Some of them had not forgiven him. Even a few of his onetime friends wanted nothing to do with him.

Yet, some of the people that knew Orlando stood by him. One of them was Octavio "Cookie" Rojas, one of Cepeda's former teammates with the Royals and now a coach with the Chicago Cubs. During Cepeda's stay in prison, Rojas had addressed a letter to the people of San Juan, Puerto Rico. In the following excerpt from the letter, he asked the people of Cepeda's homeland to give him another chance:

> *I say that if a man accepts his mistakes and can straighten out a few young lives, he is more valuable on the outside to teach others than to sit behind the walls of confinement. How can we forget all the things this man has done for his country?*
>
> *Cookie Rojas, 1978*

Rojas also sent a letter to United States President Jimmy Carter. He asked the nation's leader to grant Cepeda a pardon, which would release him from prison. President Carter didn't pardon Cepeda, but Rojas's work still paid off. Orlando's lawyer—a man named Brian David—showed a judge the letters of support that his client had received from Rojas and other people in baseball. Along with Cepeda's model behavior in prison, the letters helped convince the judge to reduce his sentence and make him eligible for parole almost right away.

Upon his release from prison, Cepeda continued to do the kind of good things that Rojas had talked about. Orlando went to work in a drug rehabilitation program at a Philadelphia halfway house. Cepeda also decided to write a letter to Bowie Kuhn, the commissioner of baseball. In the letter, he apologized to Kuhn for the way that he had disgraced himself and the game. He asked for forgiveness, pleading with the commissioner to allow him to return to baseball in some capacity. Cepeda felt that he could have a positive impact on young players by telling them about his own mistakes and offering advice on how to avoid those same problems. The letter left such an impression on Kuhn that he sent it to Dallas Green, the head of the Philadelphia Phillies' minor league system. Green decided to offer Cepeda a job as one of the team's minor league hitting instructors. Orlando gladly accepted.

Cepeda reported to Reading, Pennsylvania, where the Phillies had a Class-AA minor league team. He worked with the team's young hitters, offering them encouragement and advice. He clearly loved his return to baseball. "I have never been happier in my life," Cepeda said in an interview with the *New York Times.*

Yet, he didn't want to remain in the minor leagues indefinitely. He yearned for a job in the major leagues. Dallas Green wrote letters to other major league teams on Orlando's behalf, praising the work he had done in the Phillies' farm system. Bill Veeck, the owner and president of the Chicago White Sox, received one of the letters. He decided to offer Orlando a job as the team's major league batting instructor.

Cepeda made a quick impression on White Sox players. He urged players to use "every minute" of spring training as preparation for the regular season. "I intend to make every minute count from now on," outfielder Thad Bosley told Joe Goddard of *The Sporting News.*

Several of the White Sox's young hitters praised Cepeda for helping them improve. "He has a photographic memory of what you do at bat—right or wrong," outfielder Wayne Nordhagen told Hal Bock of the Associated Press. "He leaves you alone and doesn't try to force any of his ideas on you. But if you slump and get messed up, he can show you how to get back where you were." With Cepeda guiding him, Nordhagen enjoyed his best major league season.

Unfortunately, Cepeda didn't perform as well in other aspects of the job. The White Sox fired him after only one year. For the next three seasons, he coached and scouted in the Puerto Rican Winter League. He also achieved one of the greatest goals of his life.

Cepeda opened a baseball school in San Juan. It allowed him to instruct young Puerto Rican players, some of whom came from underprivileged families, on the finer points of the game. His students included future major league player Candido "Candy" Maldonado, who would play for the Giants and six other teams during a productive fifteen-year career.

Yet, there still existed too many negative feelings toward Cepeda in his native land. He realized that he would have to move to the United States, where sentiment was not as antagonistic toward him. In 1984, Cepeda moved to Los Angeles, where he taught American youngsters about the game that he had played so well and loved so much.

Although Orlando felt like he was doing something worthwhile, the baseball school in Los Angeles soon failed. So did his marriage to his second wife, Nydia. After too many arguments, she divorced him, taking with her the couple's four sons.

Circumstances continued to worsen for Cepeda. One day in 1984, he visited with some players prior to a game at Dodger Stadium. When a security guard discovered that he did not have a field pass, Orlando was asked to leave the ballpark. Later on, the Dodgers instructed all of their players not to speak to Cepeda, whom they considered a bad influence. Orlando Cepeda had hit rock-bottom.

Isolated from the rest of his family and rejected by baseball, Orlando stewed in his own feelings of bitterness. He dwelled too much on the negative experiences of his life, including the racism that he had faced in the United States, the ten-month sentence he had spent in prison, and the bad feelings toward him in his homeland.

Cepeda needed to improve his outlook on life, to replace the bitterness with positive feelings and energies. That improvement would come several months after a conversation with one of his friends, a musician named Rudy Regalado. Noticing how down Orlando felt, Rudy offered him a suggestion. Why not join him at one of his upcoming religious meetings? That's where Regalado practiced the religion of Buddhism.

Cepeda was a Catholic, but did not practice that religion. He agreed to attend the Buddhist meeting and liked what he heard and saw. Almost immediately, Orlando decided to convert to Buddhism.

At first, Cepeda practiced Buddhism without a great deal of enthusiasm. He then realized he had to dedicate himself fully to his newly discovered religion. The philosophies of the religion eventually worked wonders for him. Buddhism taught him that he shouldn't blame others for his own problems. He needed to take responsibility for his own misfortunes. And if he wanted to change his life, he couldn't rely on others to do the leg work for him. He would have to improve his life by making the changes on his own.

Upon discovering Buddhism, Orlando began chanting and praying regularly. He prayed that he would meet another woman, someone who would become his wife. Shortly thereafter, a mutual friend introduced him to a lady named Mirian Ortiz, who was also Puerto Rican. Mirian and Orlando would eventually marry.

The pieces of Cepeda's life were coming together. First, he had found religion. Second, he had discovered a new partner and companion. Now he needed to find another job, so that he could better support himself and his wife.

In 1987, Cepeda agreed to participate in a "fantasy camp" featuring retired players from the San Francisco Giants, his first major league team. The fantasy camp allowed older fans of the Giants to spend a few days playing baseball and mingling with some of the team's retired stars. With his friendly, down-to-earth personality, Orlando quickly became the most popular player at the Giants' fantasy camp. Most of the fans felt comfortable approaching him, whether to ask him for advice or just to make conversation. Orlando made them feel like they belonged, even though most of them had never played baseball beyond high school or college. He genuinely enjoyed talking to the fans, even though he had just met them for the first time.

Cepeda's willingness to mix with the fans did not go unnoticed by the Giants' front office. One of the team's vice-presidents, a man named Pat Gallagher, asked Cepeda if he would be interested in returning to work for his original major league team. Cepeda said yes, and the Giants eventually hired him as a "special assistant for player development." In time, Orlando became a goodwill ambassador for the team. He visited hospitals, appeared at youth camps, and delivered motivational speeches—all as a representative of the Giants.

Cepeda performed his job so well that the Giants rewarded him by asking him to throw out the ceremonial first pitch before the third game of the 1989 National League Championship Series. As a crowd of more than 62,000 fans applauded wildly, Cepeda stood on the mound at Candlestick Park and cried as he threw out the first ball. "I was crying because I knew I was where I belonged," Orlando told Ron Fimrite of *Sports Illustrated*. "Oh, it was so beautiful to be wanted again."

# Chapter Sixteen

# Waiting for the Call to the Hall

In 1993, Cepeda received some good news when he learned that he had been elected to the Puerto Rican Hall of Fame. In receiving the honor, Orlando joined the likes of Roberto Clemente in the Puerto Rican shrine. He also joined his late father, Perucho, who had been elected to the Puerto Rican Hall in 1991, its first year of existence.

For Orlando, induction into the Puerto Rican Hall of Fame represented a moment of great pride. Yet, his name remained absent from another, more prestigious Hall of Fame, whose members call Cooperstown, New York, their second home.

Once a player has retired from baseball, he must wait five years before becoming eligible for election to the National Baseball Hall of Fame, located in the small village of Cooperstown. For Cepeda, that meant he first became eligible in 1980. In order to make the Hall of Fame, a player needs to be named on at least 75 percent of the ballots cast by the baseball writers. At one point, Cepeda was considered a sure bet to receive that kind of support. Not anymore. Not after becoming involved with drugs and spending time in prison.

Year after year, Cepeda's name kept coming up on the ballot. Year after year, he kept coming up short of the votes needed for election. Well short. Year after year, the writers named him on fewer than half of the ballots.

In the early 1990s, support for Cepeda started to gain momentum. In 1994, he came closer to election than he ever had, falling only seven votes short. Unfortunately, that also marked his fifteenth and final year on the writers' ballot.

Orlando understood why he had missed out on the Hall of Fame. He felt the reasons had little to do with his performance on the field. They had much more to do with the crime he had committed during the 1970s, when he was caught smuggling drugs and later spent time in prison. Still, he felt he deserved the benefit of the doubt. "I made one mistake twenty years ago," Cepeda told Hal Bodley of *USA Today*, "and after that I have done so many wonderful things for the community and myself." He had made a successful return to major league baseball, first as a batting coach and now as a community representative for the Giants. More importantly, Orlando had worked with drug addicts in a halfway house, helped young ballplayers improve their chances of becoming successful, and lectured teenagers on the problems caused by drugs and alcohol. Cepeda felt that those accomplishments should have counted for something.

All hope of making the Hall of Fame had not been lost, however. After a three-year wait, Cepeda would once again become eligible for election to the Hall—this time through the Veterans Committee. This fifteen-man committee, which is made up of Hall of Fame players, major league executives, and longtime baseball writers, annually considers some of the outstanding players who have been passed over by the baseball writers. Cepeda was one of those players.

The Veterans Committee started looking at Cepeda's case in 1998. The committee gave him strong consideration for the Hall of Fame, but decided to elect former Negro League star Larry Doby instead. Doby deserved the honor. After a successful career in the Negro Leagues, Doby had become the first black player in American League history. He had also succeeded in overcoming much of the racism that Jackie Robinson had faced as the major leagues' first African-American player of the twentieth century.

Cepeda remained under consideration by the Veterans Committee in 1999. The committee also talked about electing several other former stars. The list included Pittsburgh Pirates' infielder Bill Mazeroski, one of the finest fielding second basemen to play the game; Boston Red Sox's center fielder Dom DiMaggio, the younger brother of the legendary Joe DiMaggio; and Cleveland Indians' pitcher Mel Harder, who won 223 games over a twenty-year career. They were all considered strong candidates; unfortunately, only one of them could be elected at a time.

On March 2, the Veterans Committee held its annual meeting in Tampa, Florida. As usual, it was a long meeting that took several hours to complete. The members of the Veterans Committee considered a number of names from the list of twentieth-century players. Many of them seemed deserving of election to the Hall of Fame. But the committee could pick only one.

Later that day, the phone rang in Orlando Cepeda's house. The voice on the other line belonged to Juan Marichal, Cepeda's teammate with the Giants from 1958 to 1966 and one of his closest friends in the game. Marichal was now a member of the Veterans Committee. He had some good news to tell his former teammate and good friend.

Family and friends, who had gathered around Orlando, let out a thunderous cheer. As Orlando continued to listen to Marichal's words, he cried. "It's hard to explain the feeling when they called me," Orlando said to the Associated Press, "and told me I was elected to the Hall of Fame." The long wait for his ultimate reward in Cooperstown, which had started after his retirement in 1974, had finally ended.

Although the wait to enter the Hall of Fame had been painful for Orlando, it also made him appreciate the honor even more. "Sometimes, when things come easy for you," he told a reporter from the Associated Press, "you tend to take them for granted." There was certainly no danger of that happening with Orlando.

In a way, entering the Hall through the Veterans Committee ranks was more special to Cepeda than election through the Baseball Writers Association of America, which consists of many young writers who didn't watch baseball in the 1950s and 1960s. "The Veterans Committee selecting me is more important than the writers," Orlando says. "I don't want to put the writers down, but many times they don't know what kind of ballplayer you were, because they never saw you play." In contrast, all members of the Veterans Committee had seen Cepeda play. "[Stan] Musial, [Ted] Williams, [Juan] Marichal, Yogi Berra, they saw me play ball. [Writers like] Bob Broeg and Allen Lewis, they saw me play, and they know what I did on the field."

More importantly, we now know what Orlando Cepeda has accomplished during his life. He has not only been rewarded with a spot in the Hall of Fame, but has made himself a better person by learning from his experiences, both the good and the bad. He has grown and matured. By admitting to his past mistakes, and discussing them freely, he has tried to help young people avoid those same pitfalls. In so doing, Orlando Cepeda has truly become one of baseball's greatest men.

## Orlando Cepeda's Career Statistics

| Year | Team | G | AB | R | H | BB | SO | HR | RBI | BA |
|------|------|---|----|----|----|----|----|----|-----|-----|
| 1958 | Giants | 148 | 603 | 88 | 188 | 29 | 84 | 25 | 96 | .312 |
| 1959 | Giants | 151 | 605 | 92 | 192 | 33 | 100 | 27 | 105 | .317 |
| 1960 | Giants | 151 | 569 | 81 | 169 | 34 | 91 | 24 | 96 | .297 |
| 1961 | Giants | 152 | 585 | 105 | 182 | 39 | 91 | **46** | **142** | .311 |
| 1962 | Giants | 162 | 625 | 105 | 191 | 37 | 97 | 35 | 114 | .306 |
| 1963 | Giants | 156 | 579 | 100 | 183 | 37 | 70 | 34 | 97 | .316 |
| 1964 | Giants | 142 | 529 | 75 | 161 | 43 | 83 | 31 | 97 | .304 |
| 1965 | Giants | 33 | 34 | 1 | 6 | 3 | 9 | 1 | 5 | .176 |
| 1966 | Giants | 19 | 49 | 5 | 14 | 4 | 11 | 3 | 15 | .286 |
| 1966 | Cardinals | 123 | 452 | 65 | 137 | 34 | 68 | 17 | 58 | .303 |
| 1967 | Cardinals | 151 | 563 | 91 | 183 | 62 | 75 | 25 | **111** | .325 |
| 1968 | Cardinals | 157 | 600 | 71 | 149 | 43 | 96 | 16 | 73 | .248 |
| 1969 | Braves | 154 | 573 | 74 | 147 | 55 | 76 | 22 | 88 | .257 |
| 1970 | Braves | 148 | 567 | 87 | 173 | 47 | 75 | 34 | 111 | .305 |
| 1971 | Braves | 71 | 250 | 31 | 69 | 22 | 29 | 14 | 44 | .276 |
| 1972 | Braves | 28 | 84 | 6 | 25 | 7 | 17 | 4 | 9 | .298 |
| 1972 | A's | 3 | 3 | 0 | 0 | 0 | 0 | 0 | 0 | .000 |
| 1973 | Red Sox | 142 | 550 | 51 | 159 | 50 | 81 | 20 | 86 | .289 |
| 1974 | Royals | 33 | 107 | 3 | 23 | 9 | 16 | 1 | 18 | .215 |
| Totals | 17 years | 2124 | 7927 | 1131 | 2351 | 588 | 1169 | 379 | 1365 | .297 |

Numbers in bold denote league-leading total

# List of Sources

## Books

*Baby Bull: From Hardball to Hard Times and Back,* by Orlando Cepeda and Herb Fagen, Taylor Publishing, 1999.
*My Ups and Downs in Baseball,* by Orlando Cepeda with Charles Einstein, Putnam, 1968.
*Orlando Cepeda,* by Laura Thorpe, Woodford Publishing.
*The Baseball Encyclopedia,* New York: MacMillian.
The Sporting News *Official 1963 Baseball Guide*
The Sporting News *Official 1968 Baseball Guide*
The Sporting News *Official 1969 Baseball Guide*
The Sporting News *Official 1970 Baseball Guide*
*Total Baseball: The Official Encyclopedia of Major League Baseball.* John Thorn, Pete Palmer, Michael Gershman, eds. New York: Harper Perennial, 1993.

## Magazines, Newspapers, and Wire Services

*Associated Press*
*Atlanta Journal*
*Baseball Digest*
*Black Sports Magazine*
*Boston Herald*
*Chicago Tribune*
*Look Magazine*
*Miami News*
*Newsday*
*New York Daily News*

*New York Post*
*New York Times*
*St. Louis Post-Dispatch*
*San Francisco Chronicle*
*San Francisco Examiner*
*Sport Magazine*
*Sports Illustrated*
*The Sporting News*
*United Press International*
*USA Today*

# Index

10/02